O9-AIE-226

WINTER IN MAJORCA

Also by Robert Graves

I, CLAUDIUS

CLAUDIUS THE GOD

COUNT BELISARIUS

SERGEANT LAMB

PROCEED, SERGEANT LAMB

WIFE TO MR. MILTON

THE GOLDEN FLEECE

KING JESUS

THE ISLES OF UNWISDOM

SEVEN DAYS IN NEW CRETE

HOMER'S DAUGHTER

WINTER IN MAJORCA

by

GEORGE SAND

WITH

JOSÉ QUADRADO'S

Refutation of George Sand

TRANSLATED AND ANNOTATED
BY
ROBERT GRAVES

VALLDEMOSA EDITION
MALLORCA

First published 1956

Printed in Great Britain

CONTENTS

ILLUSTRATIONS

MAP

FOREWORD

Un Hiver à Majorque describes a personal clash between the pre-Revolutionary Classical world and the world of post-Revolutionary Romanticism. The Romantic movement was an unstable one: an attempt to reconcile the aristocratic, mocking genius of Voltaire with the plebeian aspirations of Jean-Jacques Rousseau and the aggressive spirit of Napoleon. Its leading literary figures, most of them social misfits, had turned from the formal gardens and artificial salons of the eighteenth century to a worship of wild nature, especially in remote mountainous regions, an exploitation of ghostly mediæval terrors, and a patronage of simple, undogmatic Christianity.

George Sand (Baroness Aurore de Dudevant, *née* Dupin), the child of a *mésalliance* between an aristocrat and an ex-milliner, was the uncrowned queen of Romantics. She came to show the Majorcans by precept and example that the world had now changed, and that, by paying attention to her, they could shake themselves free from their intellectual and moral shackles, and become modern men and women. But her own house was not in order, and after a campaign of three months she retired in confusion. The precise nature of the defeat, however, is not so apparent as the bitterness it left in her heart.

The Majorcans have lately been taken to task by a leading Madrid critic, Don Torcuato Luca de Tena, Director of A.B.C., for continuing to print and sell George Sand's *Un Hiver à Majorque*, in which she brands them as barbarians, thieves, monkeys and Polynesian savages. And, indeed, they should not have let the book appear without critical comment on its many errors and hysterical slanders. Their indifference is, however, characteristically Majorcan: 'She did not like our forefathers; our forefathers did not like her. We do not change. Therefore let those who read this book judge of its truth by their knowledge of us. She must, of course, have been ill and unhappy, poor creature.'

FOREWORD

After living for a great many years in the neighbourhood which she describes, and forming a high estimate of Majorcan virtue, I am naturally interested in the historical problem of what provoked her insensate rage against the islanders. The unavoidable conclusion is that it was their part in the abrupt rejection by her lover, Frederick Chopin, of the libertarian gospel which she had taught him, and in his decision to place himself under the moral discipline of the Church. The treacherous scheming of her eight-year-old daughter Solange Sand makes a curious feature in the story.

So far as I know, no other English translation of the book has yet appeared. I have been greatly assisted by the Spanish critical edition published in 1932 by Don Gabriel Alomar, and by the help of my Majorcan friends, Don Gaspar Sabater, Don Luis Ripoll, Don Luis Alemany, Don José Maria Costa. I have also to thank Janet Seymour-Smith and Kenneth Gay for their help. And Señora de Ferrá who owns the cell, the originals of the Maurice Sand drawings here reproduced, the manuscript of *Un Hiver à Majorque* and Chopin's piano, and a great many other relics, besides being the acknowledged authority on this whole historical incident, deserves my homage as well as my thanks.

ROBERT GRAVES.

Deyá, Majorca.

WINTER IN MAJORCA

by

GEORGE SAND

AUTHOR'S NOTE

The date of this book will be found in the letter of dedication to my friend François Rollinat. The reflections which open Chapter Four are the book's justification, and I can do no better than anticipate them here: 'Why travel, unless you must?' Today, on my return from the same latitude as that of Majorca, but touched at a different point in southern Europe, I say again as I said after my visit there: 'It is not so much a question of travelling as of getting away; which of us has not some pain to dull, or some yoke to cast off?'

GEORGE SAND.

Nohant,
August 25th, 1855.

LETTER FROM A RETURNED TRAVELLER TO A FRIEND WHO STAYED AT HOME

SINCE your duties keep you at home, my dear François,[1] you believe that, borne away by the proud and wayward hobby-horse of independence, I find no more intense pleasure in the world than that of posting across seas and mountains, lakes and valleys. Alas! My sweetest, most beautiful, journeys have been made at my own fireside, feet buried in the warm embers, elbows propped on the worn arms of my grandmother's armchair. I do not doubt that your journeys are equally pleasant and a thousand times more poetic: which is why I advise you not to be too regretful of the time you waste in straining and sweating beneath tropic skies, dragging frozen feet over the snow-bound Polar plains, braving terrible hurricanes at sea, beating off the assaults of bandits, and in all similar perils and hardships which you confront in imagination every evening, without so much as taking off your slippers, and with no more serious injury than a few cigar burns in the lining of your smoking jacket.

I may perhaps reconcile you to your enforced forgoing of actual physical movement through space, by sending this account of my last journey outside France, in the certainty that you will pity rather than envy me, and will judge that too high a price can be paid for one or two transports of admiration and one or two hours of ecstasy wrested from ill-fortune. This account, written a year ago, has now earned me a most fulminating and laughable tirade of abuse from the Majorcans themselves. I am sorry that it is too long to be published as a sequel to my narrative; for the graciousness (shall we say?) with which its reproaches are worded would bear out my view of the hospitality,

[1] François Rollinat, a politician, represented Indre in the National Assembly of 1848.

good taste and tact which the Majorcans display in their dealings with foreigners.[1] This would make an admirable supporting document; but who would be able to read through to the end? And besides, since it is rather conceited and stupid to publish the compliments one earns, might it not be even worse, with things as they are nowadays, to advertise the abuse? I therefore refrain from appending the document to these pages, and confine myself to recording, as a final comment on these guileless people of Majorca, that when my account was first published, the most skilful lawyers of Palma, some forty in number, met to draw up, at the joint expense of their imagination, a terrible indictment against the 'immoral writer' who had taken the liberty of deriding their love of profit and their tender nurture of the domestic pig. We may well say, proverbially, that the whole forty felt and thought as four.[2]

But let us leave in peace these good people who were so greatly incensed against me; they have had time to calm down,

[1] Don José Quadrado wrote an article of *Vindicación* in the Palma *Diario*, which will be found in full on p. 187. He began by saying that though a few Majorcans who knew of George Sand as a writer had awaited her arrival with enthusiasm, 'her refusal to receive visits, her rudeness to a certain Marqués who had shown her many kindnesses, and the equivocal company she kept, soon made the Majorcan ladies (who preferred morality to cleverness) leave her in that solitude which she appeared to desire. . . . She came for the beauties of Nature, and found the island more lovely than Switzerland. She sought calm and solitude, and had it. She fled from journalism, and that of the modest *Diario* was all that existed in Palma. But the admiration of Europe apparently did not console her for the indifference of an obscure people.' 'Equivocal company' was George Sand's escort, Frederick Chopin, the composer. Before her association with Chopin, George Sand had formed passionate friendships with Prosper Mérimée, Alfred de Musset, Franz Liszt, Louis Michel, and others; but it was generally recognized in Paris that she was a law to herself. The final words of Quadrado's article refer to George's having brought Maurice and Solange, her two children by Casimir de Dudevant, on this illicit honeymoon—which offended Majorcan propriety—and to her suggestion (p. 115) that the monks of Valldemosa had fathered most of the villagers on local girls. 'We proclaim the truth locked in our breasts for two years past, as doubtless in many others throughout Europe, but which it is high time to publish at last: "George Sand is the most immoral of writers, and Madame Dudevant the most obscene of women."'

[2] No such event can be traced. George Sand seems to be playing on the name *Quadrado*; but the French equivalent is not *quarante*, as she seems to suppose, but *carré*.

and I to forget their manner of behaving, talking and writing. I now only recall, among the inhabitants of that beautiful island, the five or six people whose kindly welcome and friendly bearing I shall always remember as a compensation and a blessing for the hardness of my lot. If I have not mentioned them by name, this is because I do not regard myself as sufficiently important to render them famous by my gratitude; but I am certain (as I believe I say in the course of my narrative) that they too will have an affectionate enough memory of me not to believe themselves included in my disrespectful ridicule, nor to doubt the sincerity of my feelings for them.

I have told you nothing about Barcelona where, nevertheless, we spent several crowded days before embarking for Majorca. To go by sea from Port-Vendres to Barcelona in a good steamer and during fine weather is a delightful excursion. On the shores of Catalonia in the month of November we rediscovered the spring-like air which we had just been breathing at Nîmes, but which had deserted us at Perpignan; and summer heat awaited us in Majorca. At Barcelona a fresh sea breeze tempered the heat of the sun, and swept every cloud away from the wide horizon which was framed by distant mountain peaks, here black and bare, there white with snow. We made one expedition into the countryside; but the stout little Andalusian horses which conveyed us needed a good meal of oats first, if they were to fetch us smartly back under the walls of the citadel, should we come up against anything unpleasant.

You are aware that in 1838 the discontented part of the populace formed guerrilla bands and overran the whole region, barring roads, invading towns and villages, holding even the humblest dwelling-places to ransom, occupying villas as close as half a league from the town, and sallying unexpectedly from the shelter of every rock to assault the traveller with: 'Your money or your life!' We ventured, however, for several leagues along the coast, and met only some detachments of Queen Cristina's partisans on their way down to Barcelona.[1] We heard

[1] The Carlist Wars were fought between the Queen-Regent Maria Cristina, ruling for Queen Isabella, the young daughter of Fernando VII, and Don Carlos, Fernando's brother. Don Carlos, supported by the Church and the

them described as the finest troops of Spain; and thought them fine enough, and not too badly turned out, considering that they had just been on campaign. But both men and horses were so thin, the former with such gaunt and yellow countenances, the latter with such hanging heads and hollow sides, that the very sight of them made one feel hungry. The fortifications cast about the smallest hamlet saddened us even more; before the door of each poor cottage stood a modest rampart of dry stone, and a castellated tower no more solid than a piece of nougat; while loopholed walls around each roof showed clearly that no dweller in these fertile fields believed himself secure. And in many places these wretched little defences bore recent traces of attack.

Yet once through the formidable and massive fortifications of Barcelona, with a bewildering number of gates, draw-bridges, posterns and ramparts, we found nothing further to suggest that the city was at war. Behind a triple ring of cannon, and cut off from the rest of Spain by banditry and civil war, the gay youth of Barcelona sunned itself on the *rambla*, a long avenue laid out with trees and houses like our boulevards—the women, beautiful, graceful and coquettish, preoccupied by the fold of their mantillas and the play of their fans; the men by their cigars, as they strolled along, laughing, chatting, ogling the ladies, discussing the Italian opera, and seeming not to care in the least what might be happening beyond the city walls. But once night had come, when the opera had ended and the guitars fallen silent, and the city was given over to the perambulations of night-watchmen, the only sounds to be heard, above a monotonous surging of the sea, were the sentries' ominous challenges and certain still more ominous shots. These shots were fired at irregular intervals, now singly, now in rapid volleys, from various places near and far, sometimes independently, sometimes in reply, but always continuing until the first rays of the morning. Then everything returned to silence for an hour or

Conservatives, appealed to Salic Law which forbade a woman to rule Spain; Maria Cristina favoured the Liberals, and the war ended only when Mendizábal, the Liberal leader, persuaded her to let him secularize the extensive Church lands and sell them at prices which tempted enough well-to-do Conservatives to buy, and change their party coats.

two, and the well-to-do doubtless slept soundly, while the harbour woke up and the seafolk began to stir.

If, in the daylight hours of rambling and gossip, you ventured to ask what these strange and alarming night noises had meant, you were told with a smile that they were nobody's concern, and that it would be unwise to enquire into them.

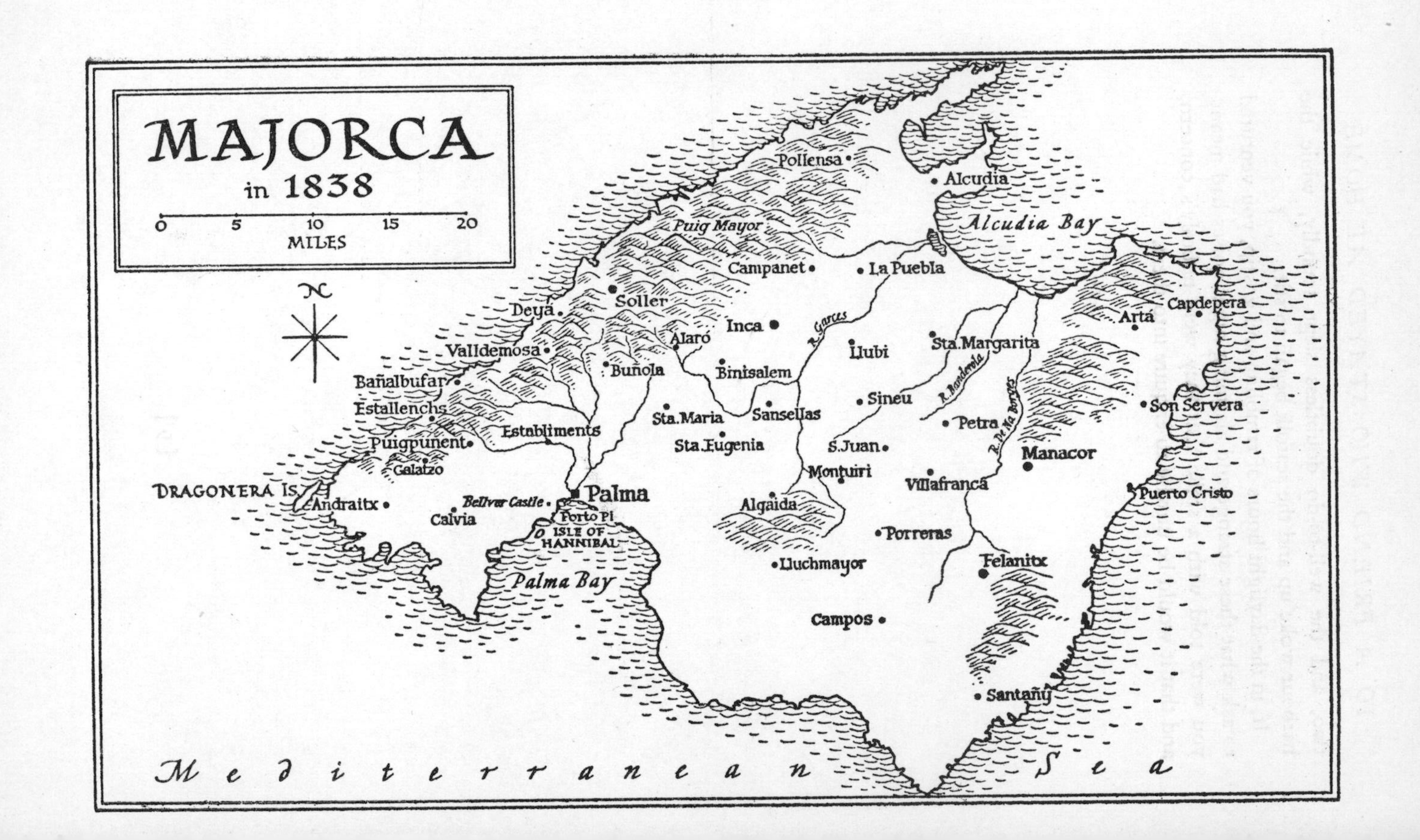
MAJORCA
in 1838
0 5 10 15 20
MILES
Pollensa
Alcudia
Alcudia Bay
Puig Mayor
Campanet
La Puebla
Soller
Deyá
Capdepera
Artá
Inca
R. Garces
Alaró
Llubi
Sta. Margarita
Valldemosa
Buñola
Binisalem
Bañalbufar
R. Banderola
Sineu
Son Servera
Estallenchs
Sta. Maria
Sansellas
Petra
R. De Na Borges
Establiments
Puigpunent
Sta. Eugenia
S. Juan
Manacor
Galatzo
Montuiri
Villafranca
DRAGONERA IS.
Andraitx
Bellver Castle
Palma
Puerto Cristo
Calvia
Porto Pi
Algaida
ISLE OF HANNIBAL
Porreras
Lluchmayor
Felanitx
Palma Bay
Campos
Santañy
Mediterranean Sea

Chapter One

IT was about a half century ago, I believe, that two English tourists discovered the valley of Chamonix, though this claim, attested by an inscription carved on a rock at the entrance of the Mer de Glace, is rather a bold one in so far as it refers to geographical discovery; these tourists (whose names I do not recall)[1] could have justified it in a sense, had they indeed been the first to draw the attention of poets and painters to the romantic landscapes where Byron conceived his wonderful *Manfred*. Generally speaking, it may be said that Switzerland was not discovered by fashionable society or by artists until the last century. Jean-Jacques Rousseau is the true Christopher Columbus of Alpine poetry and, as M. de Chateaubriand has so well observed, also the father of French Romanticism.

True, I cannot advance quite the same claims to immortality as Jean-Jacques, but when searching for something to parallel them, I find that I might have made myself as famous as the two Englishmen in the valley of Chamonix, had I claimed the discovery of Majorca. Yet the world has become so exacting that today it would not suffice for me to have cut my name on some Balearic crag: I should be expected to have produced a fairly accurate description, or at the very least a fairly poetic account of my journey that would excite tourists to make it themselves on my recommendation. But since I felt far from enraptured while in Majorca, I renounced my pioneering fame,

[1] Evidently William Wordsworth and Robert Jones, who visited the valley in 1790. At about the time that George Sand was in Majorca, Wordsworth wrote to his young friend Robert Graves: 'We went from Martigny over the Col d'Balin into Chamony, from which you explore the Mer d'Glace and as much of Mont Blanc as time and strength will allow.'

and recorded my discovery neither on granite nor on paper. Indeed, had I written under the pressure of the vexations and crosses which assailed me at that time, I should have found such boasting impossible; and every reader, on laying down my book, would have commented that I did right to refrain. Nevertheless, I make bold to confess that I was not altogether right; for artists, Majorca is one of the most beautiful places in this world, and one of the least explored. But where there is nothing except scenic beauty to describe, word-painting is so inadequate a mode of expression that I should not dream of attempting it.[1] It takes the artist's pencil and the engraver's burin to reveal Nature's splendours to lovers of foreign travel.

These long-dormant memories were aroused by a handsome book which someone laid on my desk, the other morning, entitled, *Records of an Artist's Journey to the Island of Majorca*, by J.-B. Laurens. It was with real joy that I found myself back among the palm trees, aloes, Arab buildings and Grecian costumes. I recognized all the poetically-tinted landscapes, and relived all the impressions which, I thought, had long since faded. Not a single hovel or clump of bushes failed to awake in me a world of memories (as they say nowadays); and I felt capable, if not of describing my own journey, at least of reviewing M. Laurens's. He is an intelligent and painstaking artist, works quickly and conscientiously, and must indubitably be awarded the honour forfeited by me of making the discovery in question.

M. Laurens's journey to the heart of the Mediterranean, and to coasts often as inhospitable as their inhabitants, is much more praiseworthy than the excursion to Montavert made by our two Englishmen. Nevertheless, if Europe ever became sufficiently civilized to dispense with customs officers and police, which are the external manifestations of international mistrust and dislike, and if a direct steamer service were run from France to those regions,[2] Majorca would soon prove a formidable rival to Switzerland. The journey could be made in a few days, and travellers would unquestionably find natural beauties no less

[1] But she does in Chapters six and sixteen.

[2] It now runs in the summer months: a twenty-four-hour trip from Palma to Marseilles; there are also direct air services from Paris.

delicate, and splendours no less strange and sublime than in the Alps—new pabulum for the painter.

But, though the time will doubtless come when frail dilettantes, and even lovely women, will be able to visit Palma with no more exhaustion and discomfort than Geneva, I cannot at the moment conscientiously recommend this journey except to artists of robust physique and ardent spirits.

M. Laurens had for some years acted as collaborative illustrator for M. Taylor's survey of the ancient monuments of France. Last year, left to his own devices, he decided to visit the Balearic Islands, about which he had been able to collect so little information that, as he admits, it was with a beating heart that he sailed for shores where his golden dreams might well meet with serious disillusionment. But he was destined to find what he had come to find, and to realize all his hopes—because, let me repeat, Majorca is the painter's Eldorado. Everything there is picturesque, from the peasant's hut which has preserved the traditional Arab style in the least details of its design, to the rag-swaddled child triumphant in his 'imposing uncleanliness', as Heinrich Heine says of the Veronese herb-sellers. The landscape, which is richer in vegetation than most of the North African countryside, does not yield to it in spaciousness. Simple, calm Majorca is a green Switzerland beneath a Calabrian sky, and with the silent solemnity of the Orient.

In Switzerland, the multiplicity of streams and the incessant to-and-fro of clouds give Nature's face a frequent change of colour—one might say, a continuity of movement—which painters seldom succeed in transferring to canvas; she seems to be teasing them. But in Majorca she awaits and welcomes him, moreover, the mountain vegetation, while lofty and interesting, has none of the lavishness that often blurs the outlines of a Swiss landscape. Each rocky peak stands outlined motionless against a sparkling sky, the palm tree leans over the cliff, its majestic chevelure undisturbed by the wind's caresses, and everything, down to the stunted cactus by the roadside, seems to be posing with a kind of vanity for the eye's delight.

First of all, let me give a concise description of the largest island, as if I were contributing to a gazetteer. This is by no means so easy a task as one might suppose, especially when one is forced to collect the necessary information on the spot. Spanish caution, aggravated by insular suspiciousness, forbids a foreigner to ask even the most trifling geographical question, unless he wants to be taken for a political agent. Poor M. Laurens when he dared sketch a dilapidated tower which caught his romantic eye, was arrested by the Constable on a charge of making a plan of the fortress. He writes: 'The only object that caught my attention on this coast was a dark, ochre-coloured ruin, surrounded by a cactus hedge: the Castle of Sóller. Hardly had I fixed the outlines of my sketch when four terrible, if grotesque, individuals swooped upon me. I was guilty of making, contrary to the laws of the kingdom, a plan of a fortress; and at once the fortress became a prison!

'My command of Spanish being too limited to convince these people of the absurdity of their proceedings, I had to appeal for protection to the local French Consul but, despite all his zeal, he could not get me released for three live-long hours. I was guarded by Señor Sei-Dedos ("Six-Fingers"), the Constable, a genuine Dragon of the Hesperides, and could hardly resist the temptation to hurl this comical dragon, military trappings and all, from the top of his bastion down into the sea; but on each occasion the expression on his face disarmed my wrath. Had I had Charlet's talent, I should have spent my time making studies for a caricature of this wonderfully comic fellow. Besides, I could forgive him his blind devotion to the safety of the State: since hitherto his only recreation had been smoking a cigar and staring out to sea, he naturally seized the opportunity I gave him of doing something different for a change. I returned to Sóller, heartily amused at having been taken for an enemy of the country and its constitution.'

Thereafter our traveller, determined to fill his sketch-book elsewhere than in the State prisons of Majorca, carefully limited himself to enquiries about mountain paths, and to documentary research into ruins. I should have made no more progress than he during my four months in Majorca, had I not availed myself of what little information happens to have been published by other hands. But there my perplexities began again; for the authors of these works—which are, in any case, out of date—contradict and disparage one another so haughtily, in the true tradition of travellers, that I cannot avoid rectifying certain inaccuracies, even though I may perpetrate many more. So here is my article for the gazetteer; and, to prove myself a true traveller, I shall at once assert its unquestionable superiority to all its predecessors.

Chapter Two

THE Spanish name for Majorca—which M. Laurens, like the Romans, calls *Balearis Major*, and which, according to the king of Majorcan historians, Dr. Juan Dameto, was anciently called *Clumba*, or *Columba*—is nowadays Mallorca, a corruption [of the Byzantine word *Majoricë*]; and its capital has never been named 'Mallorca', as several of our geographers are pleased to make out, but always Palma.[1]

This island is the largest and most fertile of the Balearic Archipelago, remnant of a continent whose basin must have been flooded by the Mediterranean and which, having obviously once joined Spain to North Africa,[2] shares the climate and produce of both these regions. It lies 25 leagues south-west of Barcelona, 45 from the nearest point of the African coast and, I believe, 95 to 100 leagues from the roadstead of Toulon. The total area, according to Miguel de Vargas, is 1,234 square miles, the circumference 143 miles; the greatest length, measured along the northern coast, 54 miles; and the least, measured from Palma Bay to that of Alcudia, 28 miles. The population of Majorca, which numbered 136,000 in 1787, has since risen to 160,000; during the same period, that of Palma has risen from 32,000 to 36,000.[3]

In Majorca, the temperature varies considerably with the lie

[1] No: it was called 'Mallorca' by the Moors; and by the Christians until the seventeenth century. The site of the Roman city of Palma was El Palmer, about 30 kilometres distant from the present city.

[2] No: the islands have been thrust up from the sea bed, in a slow movement of the earth's crust.

[3] Majorca lies some 100 miles from Barcelona, 180 from Algiers (the nearest point on the African coast), and about 280 from Toulon. Its population is now about 350,000; and that of Palma 150,000.

of the land and its exposure to this or that point of the compass. Summer is scorching hot throughout the plain; but the mountain chain which stretches from north-east to south-west (this direction suggesting its identity with the land masses of Africa and Spain, the nearest points of which have the same slant and fit into the same general pattern) greatly affects the winter climate. Thus de Vargas records that in the Palma streets, during a January day in the terrible winter of 1784-5, the Réaumur thermometer only once registered as few as six degrees above freezing point; on other days the temperature rose to sixteen, but the mean was eleven. Now, this temperature was more or less what we experienced in a normal winter at Valldemosa, said to be one of the coldest parts of the island. On the severest nights, when we had two inches of snow, the thermometer read six or seven degrees. By eight o'clock in the morning it had risen to nine or ten, and by midday to twelve or fourteen.[1] Usually, towards three o'clock—that is, after the sun had disappeared behind the surrounding mountain peaks—the thermometer sank suddenly to nine, or even eight, degrees. Majorca is often swept by raging north winds, and in some years the winter rains fall with an abundance and continuity of which we French have no conception.[2] On the whole, the climate is healthy and bountiful throughout the southern parts which face Africa, and which are protected from the furious Boreal squalls by a central complex of hills and the mighty escarpment of the northern range. The general plan of the island is thus an inclined plane sloping from north-west to south-east,[3] and navigation, virtually impossible in the north on account of the iron-bound coast ('precipitous and frightful, without shelter or refuge', as de Vargas records), presents no difficulties in the south.

[1] These were the average readings in the remarkably severe winter of 1953-4. George Sand's account makes it plain that the winter of 1838-9 was another of the same sort. Snow is rare in Majorca and welcomed by owners of olive groves because it kills the parasitic insects. Frost is practically unknown.

[2] Rain falls fifty days a year on an average, between October and April. There are occasional thunder-showers in the summer.

[3] No: there is a mountain range along the north-west coast, a broad central plain running parallel to this, and rolling country beyond, rising to low hills.

Despite storms and other rigours, the ancients had good reason to call Majorca the 'Golden Isle': it is extremely fertile, and its products are of excellent quality. The wheat is pure and fine enough for export to Barcelona, where this and no other is used to make the white, light pastry called *pan de Mallorca.* For their own consumption the Majorcans import a coarser and cheaper wheat from Galicia and Vizcaya, with the result that, in a land where first-class wheat grows plentifully, the bread is disgusting. I cannot say whether this transaction brings them any special advantage.[1]

In our own central provinces, which are the most backward agriculturally, farming methods display only the peasants' perseverance and ignorance. In Majorca they display much more: although the land is farmed with the most meticulous care, agriculture is in its infancy. Nowhere else have I seen the soil worked either so patiently or so ineffectually. Even the simplest machinery is unknown, and all is done by manpower: but Majorcan arms, very lean and weak compared with ours, work to an incredibly slow tempo. They take half a day to till less land than would be tilled here in two hours,[2] and five or six of the strongest men are needed to shift a load which the most diminutive of our porters would carry off gaily on his shoulders. Notwithstanding this apathy, every inch of Majorca is cultivated, and to all appearance well cultivated. The inhabitants are said never to have experienced famine; but though endowed with all the treasures of nature, and enjoying the finest of climates, they live even rougher and more grimly frugal lives than our peasants.

[1] Since the recent popularization of white flour, stomachic troubles have multiplied. The difficulty now is to buy a wholemeal loaf which has some nourishment. The old-fashioned loaf which George Sand despised made, with the addition of oil, figs, cheese and vegetables, a healthy and satisfying diet. Octogenarians and nonagenarians were common twenty years ago. It was said: 'The people here die only when they get tired of waiting.'

[2] Ploughing by oxen is not speedy even in the French Pyrenees. Ploughing a stony olive grove with a mule team, in and out of the trees, is a tricky task. There were few horses in Majorca, as George Sand explains. The peasants work long hours, and though not large-limbed are as strong as French peasants; and a great deal more sober. Owing to a 200 per cent. import tax on machinery, agriculture is still almost completely unmechanized, even on the plain.

Travellers habitually enlarge on the good fortune of the southern races, whose faces and picturesque costumes seem to reflect one long Sunday, and whose witlessness and lack of foresight they interpret as ideal rustic tranquillity. This is an error into which I myself have often fallen, but from which I am now safely delivered, especially since my visit to Majorca. No peasant in the world is so dreary and poor as this poor fellow, who can do nothing except pray, sing and work, and who never thinks. His prayer is a senseless formula that no mental effort teaches him to simplify; and his song expresses that bleak melancholy which overwhelms him in spite of himself, and the poetry of which strikes us without his being aware of its existence. Were it not that vanity occasionally arouses him from his torpor and sends him out to dance, his holidays would be consecrated wholly to sleep.

But I have already broken the literary proprieties that I set myself. Strictly speaking, the geographical essay should deal, first of all, with produce and commercial economy, and should treat only in the last paragraphs, after Cereals and Cattle, with Man.

In every descriptive geography consulted by me, the following short notice appears under the heading *Baleares*. I corroborate it here, although its detailed validity may have to be reconsidered later:

> '*These islanders are very well-disposed,* [We know that, in every island the human race falls into two categories: the cannibals and the "very well-disposed"] *gentle and hospitable. It is seldom that they commit crimes, and theft is almost unknown among them.*'

Yes, I shall certainly have to qualify these findings later on. But first of all, to discuss the produce; for I believe that in the French Chamber of Deputies certain rash (to say the least) speeches have been made envisaging our occupation of Majorca, and any member of that body who reads this book may be assumed to be far more interested by the section on produce than by my philosophic musings on the islanders' intellectual prowess.

The soil of Majorca, then, is admirably fertile, and more vigorous and scientific methods of cultivation could increase its produce tenfold. Almonds, oranges and pigs form the main exports. O lovely Hesperidean trees, guarded by foul dragons! It is not my fault that I must couple the memory of perfumed flowers and golden apples with that of those wretched porkers which cause the Majorcan owner far, oh, far more jealousy and pride; he is, after all, no more poetically inclined than the deputy whom I am addressing.

So back to my pigs. These animals, dear reader, are the finest in the world, and de Vargas, with the most guileless admiration, gives us the portrait of a young pig who, at the innocent age of one and a half years, weighed twenty-four *arrobas*, or six hundred pounds. At that time, hog-raising for profit did not enjoy the magnificent prestige which it has since won in Majorca.[1] The trade was hampered by the greed of financiers to whom the Spanish Government entrusted, which means sold, the victualling contracts. In virtue of their discretionary powers, these contractors opposed all export of livestock, while reserving for themselves the rights of unlimited import. This usurious practice tended to discourage farmers from cattle-breeding. Meat fetching so low a price, and export being forbidden, they faced ruin, and let their herds die out. The historian whom I quote laments the days of the Arab occupation, when the mountain of Artá alone grazed more head of fertile cows and noble bulls than could be rounded up today from the whole Majorcan plain.

Nor was this the only way in which the natural riches of the country were plundered. The same writer records that he remembers the mountains, and especially those of Torella and Galatzo, covered with the finest trees in the world. One olive he mentions had a girth of forty-two feet, and a diameter of fourteen;[2] but these splendid forests were despoiled by naval

[1] Majorcan black pigs are fed on beans, figs, grain and other vegetable food, never on offal or fish. Their flesh therefore is wholesome and keeps almost indefinitely in the form of dried ham, or *sobressada*—which is raw pork sausage mixed with powdered sweet pepper.

[2] An olive tree of this girth would be useless as ship's timber: the centre necessarily rotted away and the branches much cut about. It was probably a holm-oak.

carpenters, who, at the time of the Spanish expedition against Algiers, built an entire flotilla of gunboats with them. The vexations to which the owners were afterwards subjected, and the niggardliness of the damages paid, induced the Majorcans to pursue henceforth a policy of deforestation rather than afforestation. Today, the vegetation is still so plentiful and lovely that the traveller does not dream of regretting the past, but now, as formerly, in Majorca as throughout Spain, corruption is still the ruling power. The traveller, however, never hears complaints, since at the beginning of an unjust régime fear keeps the weak man silent, and when the harm has been done, he continues so from force of habit.

Although the tyranny of the contractors is at an end, Majorcan livestock has not recovered from its bankruptcy, and is unlikely to do so while export privileges are still limited to the hog trade. Very few cows and oxen are to be seen in the plain, and none at all in the mountains. Their meat is lean and tough.[1] Sheep, though of a good breed, are underfed and badly cared for; the goats, being of African stock, do not yield the tenth part of the milk that ours give.

The soil needs nourishment, and though the Majorcans lavish praise on their own agricultural methods, I still consider that the seaweed which they use for manure is a very poor fertilizer, and that their fields are far from producing what one would expect under so bountiful a sky.[2] I have carefully studied the wheat, which is so valuable that the inhabitants consider themselves unworthy of its consumption. It is identical with that raised in our central provinces, and which our peasants call white, or Spanish, wheat; and ours is no less fine, despite the difference in climate. Majorcan wheat ought, by rights, to have a marked superiority over that wrested by us from our harsh winters and unreliable springs. This is not to deny that French methods are also very crude, and that we have everything to

[1] During the past twenty years there has been a remarkable increase in dairy herds on the plain; the mountain pastures support only sheep and goats.

[2] Until the recent introduction of chemical fertilizers for the British new-potato trade, the peasants managed very well with manure and nitrogen-rich bean straw, which do not exhaust the soil.

learn in this field; but our farmer has a perseverance and an energy which the Majorcan would scorn as frenetic.

Figs, olives, almonds and oranges grow plentifully in Majorca yet, for lack of roads, the trade is far from being so extensive as it deserves. Five hundred oranges sold on the spot fetch about three francs; but to carry this bulky load on mule-back from the centre of the island to the coast would cost nearly as much again. This consideration explains the neglect of orange cultivation; these trees abound only in the valley of Sóller and in the neighbourhood of other small coves, where our fruit ships come to load. They could, no doubt, be successfully planted elsewhere: on our mountain of Valldemosa, for instance, one of the coldest parts of the island, we had splendid lemons and oranges, although they ripened later than those of Sóller. At La Granja, an estate in another mountainous region, we picked lemons as big as a man's head.[1] So far as I can make out, the island of Majorca alone could keep the whole of France supplied with these exquisite fruits, at the same price as is paid for the horrible oranges we import from Hyères and the Genoese coast. This trade, which the Majorcans boast about so much, is therefore, like everything else, kept at a standstill by their superb negligence.

A similar criticism could be made when discussing the vast produce of the olive trees, certainly the finest in the world, which the Majorcans, thanks to their Moorish inheritance, cultivate perfectly. Unfortunately, they only know how to extract a rancid and nauseating oil which would horrify us, and which they will never be able to export in bulk, except to Spain, where a taste for this contaminated oil is equally prevalent. But Spain herself has plenty of olive trees, and if Majorca provides her with oil, it must be at an extremely low price.[2] The Majorcan product is so rank that every house, man and carriage in the island, and the very air of the fields, becomes saturated with its

[1] Probably not lemons, but the large, very thick-skinned, citrus fruits with hardly any pulp, called *sidras*, used for making candied peel.

[2] The Majorcans prefer unrefined oil, which is usually delicious; every few years, however, the olives are attacked by a fly, fall before they ripen, and rot on the ground. The oil then tastes very bad. 1946 was such a year; we have had none since. George Sand was unlucky.

stench. Since no dish is prepared without oil, the effluvia rises up two or three times a day from every hearth, and the walls are steeped in it. If you lose the way when visiting the open country, you need only sniff and, if a rancid scent is wafted to your nostrils on the wings of the wind, a house will certainly be concealed behind yonder rock or clump of cacti. In the wildest and loneliest district, if this scent pursues you, raise your head; a hundred paces away you will see a Majorcan on his donkey riding down the hill towards you. This is neither a joke nor an exaggeration, but the literal truth.

The consumption of olive oil in France is enormous, the quality poor and the price exorbitant. If our method of refining were known in Majorca and, further, if Majorca had roads and, finally, if a shipping trade were organized to that particular end, we should have plenty of pure oil, whatever the severity of the winter, and at much lower prices than we now pay. I am well aware that the industrialists who grow the olive of peace in France will always prefer to sell a few tons of this precious liquid for its weight in gold, leaving our grocers to drown it in vats of peanut or colza oil and let us have the mixture at 'cost price'. Yet it would be strange if we persisted in wresting this commodity from our unkind climate, when twenty-four hours' sail away cheaper and better oil could be secured.

However, our French monopolists need not be alarmed: though we promised the Majorcans—or, for that matter, any Spaniards you please—to buy our supplies from them and multiply their riches tenfold, we could not persuade them to make the slightest alteration in their daily routine. They evince so deep a contempt for all improvements originating from abroad, and especially from France, that I doubt whether any amount of money (which they do not, on the whole, despise) would induce them to deviate in the least from their ancestral traditions.

Chapter Three

THE Majorcan, then, unable to fatten beef, or make use of wool, or milk cows (his dislike of milk[1] and butter is as profound as his scorn of industry); or grow enough wheat to dare eat bread; scarcely bringing himself to cultivate the mulberry and gather silk;[2] having also forgotten the art of carpentry, for which the island was once famous;[3] possessing no horses (since Spain still lays a maternal hand on all Majorcan colts, and takes them for her armies, the pacific Majorcan is not so foolish as to keep the kingdom in cavalry at his own expense); nor considering it necessary to maintain one single negotiable road or path in the entire island (because the export rights were left to the whims of a government too busy to concern itself with such a trifling deficiency): vegetated for a century or more, with nothing whatever to do except tell his beads and patch his breeches, which were in a sorrier state than those of Don Quixote, his prototype in poverty and pride—until the hog arrived to save the situation. Its export was declared legal, and the new era of prosperity began. In centuries to come the Majorcans will call this the Age of the Hog—just as Moslem historians celebrate the Age of the Elephant.

Olive and carob cumber the land no longer,[4] the cactus-fig no

[1] They have only recently overcome their prejudice against cow's milk, which they inherited from the Greeks and Romans; but have always milked goats and sheep.

[2] The Majorcans had a flourishing silk industry which died only at the beginning of this century, unable to compete against the Lyons manufacturers.

[3] This continued without interruption throughout the nineteenth century.

[4] Olive-growing is confined to the mountains and hills; the plain is given over to cereals, vines, potatoes and immense almond plantations.

longer serves as a plaything for children, and mothers of families have learned to economize in beans and potatoes. The pig allows no waste, he lets nothing be lost; and is the finest example of prodigal voracity, combined with simplicity of tastes and habits, that can be offered to the nations of the world. Hence he came to enjoy in Majorca rights and privileges which nobody had so far dreamed of offering to humans. Houses have been enlarged and ventilated; the fruit which used to rot on the ground has been gathered, sorted and stored; and steamships, previously considered needless and unreasonable, now run between Majorca and the mainland.

It was therefore entirely thanks to the hog that I could visit the island; had I entertained the idea of going there three years before, the prospect of so long and hazardous a journey by coaster would have made me abandon it. But, with the export of hogs, civilization has made its impression on Majorca. A handsome little steamer was bought in England which, though not built to defy the dreadful north winds that blow in Balearic waters, yet, when the weather is calm, weekly conveys two hundred pigs to Barcelona, and a few passengers as well.

It is pleasant to watch with what tender solicitude these gentlemen (I am not referring to the passengers) are treated on board, and how affectionately they are put ashore. The captain of the steamer[1] is a most agreeable man who, as a result of living and conversing with such noble creatures, has adopted their exact vocal tones and even some of their unselfconsciousness. If a passenger complains of the noise they make, the captain tells him that it is the sound of minted gold rolling on the counter. If a woman is squeamish enough to notice the stench that pervades the ship, a husband is there to remind her that money smells pretty good and that, without hogs, she would have no silk dresses, no French hats, no Barcelonese mantillas. If anyone feels sick, he need not expect the least attention from the crew; for hogs too are subject to seasickness, and in their case the malady is attended by a splenetic languor and a distaste for

[1] The steamer was *El Mallorquin*, Captain Sebata, known as 'The Peasant' because of her figure-head, a Majorcan in regional costume. She made the crossing in about eighteen hours.

life that must be combated at all costs. Forswearing all pity and humanity in order to save the lives of his beloved clients, the captain in person, armed with a whip, plunges into their midst. He is followed by the sailors and cabin-boys, each snatching up whatever lies to hand, whether an iron bar or a rope end, and in a moment the whole herd, which were lying inertly on their sides, are given a fatherly hiding, forced to rise, moved around, and counteract by violent exercise the baneful influence of the ship's rolling or pitching.

On our return journey to Barcelona, in the month of March, it was stiflingly hot, yet we were unable to set foot on deck. Even had we braved the danger of having our legs lopped off by some bad-tempered hog, the captain would never, I am sure, have allowed us to annoy them by our presence. They remained quiet at first; but, about midnight, the pilot noticed that they were sleeping very dejectedly, in the grip, it seemed, of a black depression. So the whip was prescribed, and regularly, every quarter of an hour, we were woken by such terrible cries and shrieks—of pain and rage from the beaten hogs, of inspired encouragement from the captain to his men, and of emulous oaths from the latter—that on several occasions we believed the hogs to be devouring the crew.[1]

When the ship cast anchor, we certainly hoped for a speedy farewell to such queer company, and I admit that the islanders had begun to bore me almost as much as their charges; but we were permitted to take the air only after the disembarkation of the livestock. We might have died of suffocation in our cabins, without anyone caring in the least, so long as a single hog remained to be rescued from the rolling ship and set ashore.

Sea travel has no terrors for me, but a member of my family was dangerously ill.[2] During the crossing, the foul stench and the lack of sleep had not helped to relieve his sufferings. The only attention paid us by the captain was a request not to put

[1] A fancy tale of George Sand's. The sound of beating was probably the whacking noise of the waves against the sides of the ship, once the southern headland had been cleared.

[2] Frederick Chopin. His name is never mentioned in this book. He was then twenty-eight. George Sand was thirty-four; her son Maurice was fifteen, her daughter Solange eight.

our invalid in the best bed of the cabin, because the Spanish have a superstition that every disease is infectious,[1] and since the captain had already decided to burn the bed in which the invalid slept, he naturally wanted it to be the worst one. We returned him to his hogs; and a fortnight later, on our way home in *Le Phénicien*, a splendid steamer flying our flag, we compared the Frenchman's devoted attention with the Spaniard's notion of hospitality. The captain of *El Mallorquin* had grudged a bed to one who appeared to be dying; the Marseilles captain, thinking his accommodation inadequate, had lent him the mattress off his own bed. . . . When I wanted to settle for our passage, the Frenchman informed me that I was offering him too much; the Majorcan had made me pay double.

My conclusion is not that man is wholly good in one corner of our 'terraqueous globe', or wholly bad in another. Bad character, among humans, is caused by material ills. Suffering engenders terror, mistrust, deceit, every sort of conflict. The Spaniard, being ignorant and superstitious, believes in infection, fears illness and death, lacks faith and charity. Being also wretched and ground down by taxation, he becomes greedy, selfish, and dishonest in his dealings with foreigners. History teaches us that whenever he has been given the opportunity to be great, he has displayed greatness. But he is only human, and where in private life a man must give way, he gives way.

I need to lay down this principle before going on to speak of humanity as I found it in Majorca; for I hope I am excused any further discussion of olives, cows and pigs. The very length of this last essay displays rather bad taste. Apologizing to anyone whose feelings may be wounded by it, I shall now settle down seriously to my narrative. At first it appeared that my sole task would be to follow M. Laurens step by step in his Artistic Journey, but I can already see how many different reflections will plague me as I retrace in memory the rough paths of Majorca.

[1] Chopin insisted that he had an ordinary bronchitis, though one of his sisters had already died of consumption, then an incurable disease, and consumption had been correctly diagnosed in his own case by the Palma doctors.

Chapter Four

'BUT since you know nothing about painting,' I shall be asked in Molière's words, 'what the deuce were you doing in that gallery?' Here I prefer to discuss my family and myself as little as possible; though I shall often be obliged to use the words *I* and *we*. 'I' and 'we' represent that accidental subjectivity without which certain aspects of Majorcan life, interesting perhaps to the reader, would not have presented themselves objectively. In this context therefore I beg everyone to consider my personality as something altogether passive, a telescope for observing scenes in distant lands that invite the catch-phrase: 'I would rather believe you than go there and see. . . .' Moreover, it is not my wish to beguile him with the accidents that befell me. If I recall them, this will be merely in illustration of a philosophical theme; and when it has been advanced and argued, the reader will do me the justice of acknowledging that I am not in the least egocentric.

But let me tell my reader without further ado what I was doing there: 'I wanted to travel.' And now it is my turn to ask him a question: 'When you travel, dear reader, why do you travel?'

I hear him reply, in the very words that I myself would choose: 'I travel for the sake of travelling.'

'Travel is admittedly an end in itself; but still, what impels you to this costly and exhausting pleasure, sometimes dangerous and always strewn with disillusions?'

'The need to travel.'

'There you are! But what is this need? Why are we all haunted by it to a greater or lesser degree? Why do we all give way to it, even after realizing time and time again that, as soon as we are in the saddle, the need also scrambles up behind and will neither relax its grip on us nor allow any place we approach to give us satisfaction?'

Since my reader refuses to answer this question, I shall be honest enough to do so myself. The fact is that nowhere, these days, is anyone genuinely happy, and that of the countless faces assumed by the Ideal—or, if you dislike the word, the concept of something better—travel is one of the most engaging and most deceitful. All is rotten in public affairs: those who deny this truth feel it even more deeply and bitterly than those who assert it. Nevertheless, divine Hope still pursues her way, assuaging our tormented hearts with the constant whisper: 'There is something better—namely, your ideal!'

Our social order does not even command the sympathies of its defenders; each of us in dissatisfaction chooses whatever escape suits him best. One throws himself into art, another into science, the majority stupefy themselves with whatever comes nearest to hand. All of us who have time and money to spare, travel—that is to say, we flee; since surely it is not so much a question of travelling as of getting away? Which of us has not some sorrow to dull, or some yoke to cast off? My contention is that nobody, unless either engrossed in work or numbed by idleness, can stay for long in one place without becoming ill-at-ease and wanting a change. Every happy person (though only the very great and the very indolent qualify for this title nowadays) expects to become still happier by travelling; do not as many lovers and newly-married couples set out for Switzerland or Italy as do idlers and hypochondriacs? In a word, anyone who feels himself either alive or rotting away catches the fever of the Wandering Jew and rushes off in search of some remote nest for love-making, or of some remote hole for self-burial.

Heaven forbid that I should inveigh against popular migration, or imagine that in a reformed future men will remain glued to their country, their plot of land, and their house, like polyps to a sponge! Yet if intelligence and morals are to advance hand in hand with industry, railways are clearly not destined to shuttle from one end of the earth to the other entire nations suffering from spleen or morbid restlessness. I should like to envisage the human race as happier, hence calmer and more enlightened, and leading two complementary lives: a sedentary life of devotion to a happy home, work in the city, study and philosophical meditation; and an active life, of devotion not only to the honest exchange which will one day replace the shameful traffic we call commerce, but to inspirations of art, to scientific research and (above all) to the broadcasting of ideas. In a word, I see the natural end of travel as a satisfaction of the need for contact, communication and the congenial interchange of ideas—pleasure should coincide with duty. Nowadays, on the contrary, most of us seem to travel for the sake of mystery or isolation, yet under a shadow with which the society of our fellow-beings clouds all impressions, be they sweet or painful.

I set out in order to satisfy a need for repose which I was feeling more keenly than usual. Since in this world that we have made for ourselves time is always short, I fancied once again that I should find some faraway quiet retreat where there would be no notes to write, no newspapers to peruse, no callers to entertain; where I could always wear my dressing-gown, where every day would last for twelve hours, where I could shake off the duties of polite behaviour, break away from the mental turmoil by which we French are all tormented, and devote a year or two to a little historical research, and to studying the grammar and syntax of my own language at the same time as my children.[1]

Who has not indulged in this selfish dream of disappearing one fine morning, of abandoning his affairs, his habits, his acquaintances and even his friends, to settle in some enchanted island and live without worries, without commitments and, finally, without newspapers? It is no figure of speech to say that the Press, that first and last of things, as Æsop would have called it, has created for man an entirely new life, replete with

[1] She went to Majorca mainly to enjoy her secret love-affair with Chopin, beyond reach of the censorious Paris society; Chopin himself had religious scruples about their relationship, and feared that his pupils, family and fashionable hostesses might come to know of it. Both also hoped to work without interruption: she on revising her *Lélia* and writing her mystical religious novel *Spiridion*, he on his piano compositions.

progress, privileges and cares. This voice of humanity which wakes us up every morning to inform us how humanity lived yesterday, sometimes publishing great truths, sometimes terrifying falsehoods, but always recording every step taken by humankind, and chiming every hour of social life, is surely a pretty big thing, despite all the blemishes and ills associated with it? But though the Press is necessary for the clarification of our thoughts and the control of our deeds, are its readers not shocked and bored, in an epoch of general conflict, to count the weeks and months of continual abuse and threats, which pass without any light being thrown on a single question, or any perceptible progress being registered? And in this period of waiting, which seems all the longer because every one of its phases is scrupulously reported to us, are we not often seized with the desire—we artists who have no control over the helm—to fall asleep in the ship's scuppers and not wake up for several years, until we may hail the new coastline towards which we find ourselves borne?

Yes, indeed, if only we could thus stand aside from communal life for awhile, renouncing every contact with politics, we should doubtless be struck on our return with the progress achieved during our absence. But this is not granted us, and when we flee from the scene of action to seek oblivion and rest among some nation of slower pace and less passionate spirit than ours, we suffer ills that we could not have foreseen: we regret having deserted the present for the past, the living for the dead.

Such quite simply is the theme of this book, and my reason for attempting the far from pleasant task of writing it. And although I promised myself, when I began, to dispense as much as possible with personal impressions, I now see that such an evasion would be an act of cowardice, and consequently withdraw my promise.

Chapter Five

We reached Palma early in the month of November, 1838, and found the heat there comparable to that of a French June. Since it had been extremely cold in Paris a fortnight before, we were delighted after experiencing the first assaults of winter to have apparently left the enemy behind. To this pleasure was added that of exploring a town with a distinct character of its own, and one which contained several buildings in the first rank of beauty or historical interest.

However, the difficulty of finding accommodation soon obtruded itself, and we found that the Spaniards who had recommended Majorca to us as the most hospitable and well-supplied island in the world had, like ourselves, been labouring under a great delusion.[1] Who would have guessed that, in a country so close to civilized Europe, we should be unable to find a single inn?[2] This lack of even temporary accommodation for travellers ought to have warned us, once and for all, how Majorca compared with the rest of the world, and sent us straight back to Barcelona where, at least, there is one wretched inn emphatically named the Hotel of the Four Nations. At Palma, one has to carry letters of introduction and recommendation to twenty of the more important local personages, who have been given several months' warning, unless one can face the prospect of sleeping in the open air. The most we could do was to secure a couple of small semi-furnished rooms in a disreputable quarter

[1] Martini, the Spanish Consul in Paris, and Mendízábal, the Liberal leader.

[2] In out-of-the-way towns and villages of Majorca the paucity of inns is still noticeable; there are not enough tourists or commercial travellers to make them pay.

of the town[1] where a stranger is lucky if he can find a trestle-bed with a mattress little more downy and resilient than a slate, a straw-bottomed chair, and a menu dominated by sweet pepper and garlic.

There less than an hour's stay taught us that, unless we professed to be delighted by this reception, we should either earn black looks as impertinent blunderers or, with better luck, pitying stares as idiots. Woe betide the traveller in Spain who is not pleased with everything he encounters! Make the slightest grimace on finding vermin in a bed, or scorpions in the soup, and you draw upon yourself universal scorn and indignation. So we took good care never to complain, and gradually came to understand the reasons for the lack of comfort and the apparent lack of hospitality. Quite apart from the habitual listlessness of the islanders, the Civil War, which had so long convulsed Spain, was now suspending normal traffic with the mainland. Majorca had become the refuge of as many Spaniards as it could house, and the natives, securely entrenched in their homes, were chary of leaving them to search for adventures and hard knocks overseas.[2] Then there was the absence of any industrial activity, and the inordinate customs duty levied on all comforts and luxuries. To give an example: for a piano which we had sent from France, we were asked to pay 700 francs import duty, which was practically the value of the instrument. We tried to send it back, but this was forbidden; to leave it at the port until further notice was equally forbidden; to have it moved out of the town (we were then living in the country) and thereby avoid at least the harbour dues, which differ from the customs dues, was illegal; to leave it in the town, and thereby avoid the exit dues, which are different from the entrance dues, was impossible; all that we had the right to do was throw it into the sea. After a fortnight's

[1] The Calle de la Marina, the main street leading to the port. They stayed in this lodging-house for a week and then left because it was over a cooper's shop and the din of hammers prevented George Sand from working.

[2] The Majorcans, though almost Taoist in their dislike of foreign wars and domestic brawls, are hardy seamen; devoted smugglers; and as they proved in August 1936 when Captain Bayo's Catalans landed at Puerto Cristo, most resolute in defence of their homes. Even the women came out with their pig-killing knives and pitchforks.

haggling, we won the concession that instead of being taken out of the town by one gate, it should be taken out by another, and so got away at the cost of some four hundred francs.[1]

Palma is designed to hold only a certain number of inhabitants; as the population increases, they huddle a little closer together. Hardly any new houses are built. Nothing is altered in their homes: with the exception of a very few families, no one owns furniture of a type more modern than two centuries ago.[2] There is a general ignorance of fashion, and no desire for luxury, or even for the amenities of life. Hedged in by their own apathy on one hand, and external obstacles on the other, they possess no more than is needed for their personal use. Hence hospitality, which implies superfluity, is in practice limited to courteous phrases.

The formula used in Majorca, and throughout Spain, if one wants to excuse oneself from lending anything, is the grandiloquent, 'This house and all its contents are at your disposal.' One cannot look at a picture, finger a piece of material, or lift up a chair, without being told most charmingly: '*Es*[*tá*] *a la disposición de Usted.*' But beware of accepting so much as a pin: that would be a flagrant impropriety. In my early days at Palma I was guilty of a breach of good manners and, I am sure, my spirit will never recover from the shame. Having brought a letter of unimpeachably noble introduction to a young marquis there,[3] I thought that I could accept his carriage (so charmingly had the offer been made) and go for a drive! But next day a note from him made it quite plain that I had violated the proprieties, and I hastened to send his turnout back unused.[4] I did indeed come across exceptions to this rule, but only among Majorcans who had acquired a knowledge of the world by travel

[1] Import difficulties of this sort still exist because Spanish revenues depend largely on tariffs. But the system is not so rigid as it appears, and the authorities, if courteously and reasonably addressed, are willing to stretch a point wherever they will not get into trouble themselves by so doing.

[2] Some old Palma houses are still furnished almost throughout in seventeenth-century style.

[3] The Marquis of La Bastída.

[4] There seems to have been a misunderstanding, if this is the occasion to which Don José Quadrado refers in his *Vindicación*, published in the Palma *Diario* two years later; he says that she was unpardonably rude to a marquis who had shown her many kindnesses (see p. 187).

and were true cosmopolitans. And, so be it only to establish the straitened circumstances to which import-dues and lack of industry have reduced so rich a country, I must add that even if any of the others were prompted to kindliness by the nobility of their hearts, not one of them could have made over a corner of his house to us without experiencing inconveniences and even hardships which we should have been grossly tactless to impose on a stranger.

We were in a better position to appreciate the obstacles that confronted them, when looking for somewhere to live ourselves. Not a single habitable flat was available in the entire city. A Palma flat consists of roof, floor and bare walls, without doors or windows. In most middle-class houses window-panes are not used; and anyone wishing to provide himself with this comfort, essential in winter, must first get the frames made. Each tenant, therefore, when he moves (which happens very seldom) takes the windows, the locks, and even the hinges of the door away with him. His successor must begin by replacing these, unless he has a taste for living in the open, which is quite a common one in Palma.[1]

Now, it takes at least six months to get doors and windows made, not to mention beds, tables, chairs and all similar furnishings, however plain and primitive. There are few carpenters; they do not work quickly; tools and materials are hard to come by, and the Majorcan always finds some good reason why he should not hurry. Life is so long! Only the French, that is to say the extravagant and hysterical, want things done at once. 'If you have already waited six months, should you not wait another six months? If you do not like the island, why stay? Are you needed here? We were managing well enough without you. And do you imagine that you are going to set everything at sixes and sevens? Oh no, indeed! We let you talk of course, but we do as we please.'

[1] In 1934 I bought the guest-house that had belonged to the former squires of Deyá, the nearest village to Valldemosa: a noble building in the angle between the Church and the Rectory. Of the eight rooms, only two bedrooms were glazed. Several cottages in the village had no glass at all, and the old women used to sit spinning on their thresholds in all weathers. Their daughters and grand-daughters are not nearly so hardy.

'But have you anything to hire?'

'Hire? What do you mean? Hire furniture? Do you imagine that we have enough to spare for hiring?'

'Or anything for sale?'

'For sale? You mean ready made? Do you imagine we can afford to make furniture before anyone asks for it? Why not have what you need sent from France—if it is true that you can get everything there?'

'But that would mean waiting at least six months, and then paying duty. Do you mean to tell me that if anyone has been foolish enough to come here, his only means of repairing the mistake is to go away again?'

'That is what I should suggest. That, or to have patience, great patience.' *Mucha calma* epitomizes Majorcan wisdom.[1]

We were about to act on this advice and return to France, when some thoroughly well-meaning person did us the bad turn of finding a country place which we could rent.[2] It was the villa of a rich townsman who, for one hundred francs a month —a very moderate price, by French standards, but high enough by theirs—made it over to us just as it stood. It was furnished like all Majorcan country houses: with camp-beds or wooden ones painted green, often consisting simply of two trestles supporting a couple of boards and a thin mattress; straw-bottomed chairs; rough wooden tables; bare but immaculately whitewashed walls and, as a crowning luxury, glazed windows in almost every room. The so-called drawing-room contained four dreadful fire-screens, like those found in our poorest village inns, which Señor Gomez, our landlord, had been simple-minded

[1] Visitors to London at the conclusion of the Second World War found much the same situation; hotels full, no flats, and even the cheapest furniture selling at extravagant prices. A long war, shortage of raw materials, shrinking of imports, and crowds of refugees account for the inability of the Palma carpenters—in the days before saw-mills—to supply immediately what was asked. This is not to deny that Majorcan carpenters habitually undertake more work than they can possibly finish by the dates promised. But theirs is a form of optimism tnat one learns to expect and forgive. And if ever there is obvious need for immediate work—a coffin, a nuptial bed for a wedding, or a worm for an olive-press—the task will be done even if the carpenter has to work all hours.

[2] Son Vent (House of the Wind) is still standing at Establiments, down a winding lane off the Palma road.

enough to get carefully framed, as though they were valuable engravings, to form mural decorations for his country-seat. The villa was palatial, well-ventilated (too much so), well laid out, and most agreeably situated, among the fertile foothills of the mountains and at the far end of a rich valley that runs down towards Palma's yellow walls, massive cathedral, and the sparkling sea stretched beyond.

Our first days in this haven passed pleasantly We went for strolls, revelling in the delightful climate and a countryside fascinatingly new to us. Although I have spent a great part of my life on the road, I had never been very far from my own country. This was my first experience of a land whose vegetation and natural features differed radically from those presented by our colder latitudes. When I visited Italy and stepped out upon the Tuscan beaches, the highly coloured picture that my imagination had painted of this region prevented me from appreciating their pastoral beauty and their smiling charm. I walked along the banks of the Arno, and it might have been my own river Indre; and travelled as far as Venice without finding any occasion for surprise or emotion. But in Majorca I could make no comparison with any remembered place. The people, the houses, the plants, the very pebbles on the road, had a distinct character of their own. My children were so struck by it that they collected everything, and wanted to fill our trunks with those beautiful blocks of quartz and veined marble which are built into the dry-stone walls of every enclosure Some of the peasants who saw us gathering even dead twigs mistook us for apothecaries; others for simple lunatics.

Chapter Six

SHAKEN and distorted by later cataclysms than those that formed the primitive world, the island of Majorca offers a rich variety of landscape. The district where we were now living, called Establiments, encloses widely differing scenery within a horizon of a few leagues. Immediately around us, cultivation was confined to a system of broad, unsymmetrical terraces following the contours of the foothills that merged with the fertile plain. Terrace farming, common throughout the island (which is continually threatened by rain and sudden torrential floods) greatly benefits the trees and makes the countryside appear like a beautifully-kept orchard. To the right of our house, the hills rose progressively from the gently-sloping pasture to fir-fledged crags. A stream skirts the mountains in winter, and occasionally runs after summer thunderstorms, though when we arrived it was still little more than a bed of untidy boulders. But the handsome mosses which overgrew the boulders; the little bridges, green with damp, split by the force of past currents and half hidden by the branches of willows and poplars; the intertwining of these slender and tufted trees, as they overhung the river-bed to cradle it in greenery from bank to bank; the thin trickle of water running soundlessly among the rushes and the myrtles, and the eternal group of children, women and goats huddled on the mysterious embankments—all such pictorial riches clamoured for the painter's brush. We used daily to walk along the bed of the stream, and called this wilder part of the landscape 'Poussin's Own' because its elegance and melancholic pride reminded us of the places that he particularly loved.

A few hundred yards from our hermitage, the torrent split

into several streams, and seemed to lose itself in the plain. Olives and carobs spread their branches above the cultivated land, and gave it the look of a forest. On the many round hillocks fringing this wooded area rose cottages of great distinction, although Lilliputian in size. One could never believe how many barns, sheds, stables, court-yards and gardens a *pagés* (peasant) manages to crowd into an acre of land, and what natural good taste presides over this seemingly whimsical lay-out. Most cottages consist of two storeys and a gently-tilted tiled roof, the eaves of which protect a perforated loft; as it were a row of battlements roofed in Florentine style. This symmetrical crown lends an air of majesty and strength to the flimsiest and poorest buildings, and the huge sheaves of maize hung at every aperture of the loft, make [with long strings of tomatoes and red peppers][1] a heavy garland of alternating amber and red, the effect of which is unbelievably opulent. Around this cottage usually rises a strong hedge of cactus, or nopal, whose queer racquet-shaped growths combine to screen the meagre reed-and-rush sheep pens and keep out the cold winds. Since these peasants never rob one another, this is the only barrier that encloses their estates. Almond trees and orange thickets surround the gardens where hardly any vegetables grow except red peppers and tomatoes; but all is superbly coloured, and often, to set off the picture, one lonely palm tree unfolds its elegant parasol above the cottage, or leans gracefully across, like the aigrette in a hat.

Establiments is one of the most prosperous districts of Majorca, and the reasons given by M. Grasset de Saint-Sauveur in his *Journey to the Balearic Islands* confirm my remarks about the general inadequacy of Majorcan cultivation. The observations on the apathy and ignorance of the local *pagés*, made while an Imperial officer in 1807, led him to investigate their causes. He found two main ones. The first, namely the great number of religious establishments, absorbing a large proportion of the limited population,[2] no longer exists thanks to M. Mendizábal's draconic decree; yet the devout of Majorca will never forgive him for it. The second was the prevailing menial mentality,

[1] This explanatory phrase has dropped out of the original edition.

[2] Some 750 monks and 350 nuns.

which herded sturdy young people together by the score in the service of the wealthy and well-born. This evil still flourishes: every Majorcan aristocrat has a more numerous retinue than he can afford to retain, though he derives no benefit from it whatsoever; nor could he possibly be worse attended than by this kind of honorary servant. When one wonders how a rich Majorcan can spend his income in a country bare of all luxuries and temptations, the answer is found in the houseful of good-for-nothing loafers of both sexes, who occupy a wing of his mansion set aside for this purpose, and as soon as they have spent one year in his service, enjoy the right to be lodged, clothed and boarded for the rest of their lives. Those who wish to excuse themselves from this serfdom may do so by resigning certain benefits; but custom sanctions their continued morning visits to take chocolate with their former comrades, and their sharing, like Sancho at Gamache's residence, in all the festivities of the household.

At first sight these customs appear patriarchal, and one is tempted to admire the republican spirit ruling the relations between master and man; but one soon recognizes it as an ancient Roman type of Republicanism. These servants are clients fettered by sloth or pennilessness to the vanity of their patrons. The Cavallers of Majorca esteem it a luxury to employ a staff of fifteen in an establishment that would call for two at the outside.[1] And when one sees great stretches of land lying fallow,[2] industry in ruin, and all advanced ideas proscribed by stupidity and sloth, one is at a loss to know who deserves the greater contempt: the master who thus sponsors and perpetuates the

[1] This habit lasted until about fifty years ago, despite the gradual impoverishment of the Cavaller families. The large palaces of Palma which still remain in their possession now have most of their immense, tapestry-hung rooms locked up, for lack of staff; only when a death occurs are they opened and footmen hired to dress in the family livery and revive the good old days. I visited one of them recently; a single man-servant in charge spoke vaguely of his companions who were out in the country helping with the harvest. He showed me the library with its cracked ceiling, ill-fitting windows and broken chairs: the shelves held about five thousand volumes—priceless incunabula rubbing shoulders with mid-nineteenth-century post-card albums and fashion magazines.

[2] She is referring perhaps to the huge game preserves; there are still many such in the island. Rabbit and partridge abound, but no larger quarry.

moral degradation of his fellows, or the serf who prefers a humiliating leisure, to work which would earn him an independence consonant with the dignity of mankind.

It happened once, however, that certain rich Majorcan landowners, observing that their expenses were on the increase and their assets on the wane, owing to the laziness of their employees and the shortage of labour, decided on a remedy. They leased part of their estates to selected peasants on a life tenure, and M. Grasset found that, wherever this measure was tried, the earth which had hitherto seemed cursed with barrenness, brought forth in such plenty, because the labourers had an interest in its improvement, that after a few years both contracting parties found their financial situation eased.[1]

M. Grasset's prophecies on this head have been completely fulfilled, and today the district of Establiments, among others, has become an immense garden; its population has increased, numerous new dwelling places have been erected on the small hills, and the peasants have won a reasonable standard of living which, though it has not greatly enlightened them, at least increases their capacity for work. It will be many years until the Majorcan becomes energetic and industrious; and if, like us French, he must first pass through the distressing stage of the private profit motive before he can learn that this is still not the goal of humanity, we may well allow him meanwhile to kill time with his guitar and his rosary. But doubtless a better fortune than ours lies in store for these infant nations, whom we are destined to initiate into a truly civilized existence without grudging them the benefits we confer. They are not sufficiently strong to face the revolutionary storms raised around us by the sense of our perfectibility Alone, disowned, mocked and fought against by the rest of the earth, we French have made enormous progress; yet the noise of our gigantic struggles has not broken the profound slumber of the small nations living within range of our cannon in the heart of the Mediterranean. A day will come when we shall bestow on them the baptism of true liberty, and they will sit down at the feast, like labourers engaged at the eleventh hour to work in the vineyard. Let us discover the secret

[1] A fifty-fifty profit-sharing system is now general.

of our social destiny, let us fulfil our lofty dreams; and while the nations about us enter gradually into our revolutionary church, these unfortunate islanders, whose weakness perpetually exposes them as a prey of the savage powers who fight around them, will flock to join our communion.[1]

Until the time when France shall be the first people in Europe to decree universal equality and independence for all, the world must still be ruled by the strongest armies or the most cunning diplomats; international law is a mere phrase, and the only prospect facing such isolated minorities as 'The Transylvanian, Turk or Magyar'[2] is to be engulfed by a conqueror. Were no better future in store for Majorca, I should not wish Spain, England or even France to be her guardian, but should take as little interest in the fortuitous issue of events as in the queer brand of civilization that we are now exporting to Africa.

[1] Majorca had, however, contrived to keep its independence (though the title 'King of the Balearics' became swallowed up in 'King of Spain') since the year 1229; and still keeps it. The doubtful benefits of French culture are to be seen in towns and villages made over-prosperous by close ties with the French fruit trade.

[2] La Fontaine: *Fable of the Thieves and the Ass.*

Chapter Seven

We had spent three weeks at Establiments before the rains began.[1] Hitherto the weather had been enchanting; the lemon trees and myrtles were still in flower, and once, early in December, I stayed out on a terrace until five o'clock in the morning, and kept deliciously warm. You may trust me when I say that the temperature was high because I have never met anyone who feels the cold so much as I do, or whose enthusiasm for the beauties of Nature is more readily dulled by the slightest feeling of chilliness. Besides, for all the charm of the scented and moonlit landscape, my vigil was not an exacting one: I was no poet in search of inspiration, but an idler with ears and eyes wide open to catch and account for the noises of the night.

It is a commonplace that each country has its harmonies, its groans, its cries, its mysterious whisperings, and this nocturnal language of material things is by no means the least of the distinctive signs which strike the traveller. The mysterious lapping of water against the cold marble slabs of the Grand Canal palaces, the heavy measured tread of *sbirros* on the quay, the shrill and almost childlike cry of mice chasing one another and wrangling on the muddy paving stones, in short all the stealthy and curious noises that faintly disturb the dreary silence of a Venetian night, bear no resemblance whatsoever to the monotonous sound of the sea the *¿quien vive?* of the sentries, and the melancholy song of the *serenos*, or night-watchmen, of Barcelona. The harmonies of Lake Maggiore differ from those of the Lake

[1] This will not have been earlier than December 7th, since they came to Son Vent on November 15th. The weather breaks in most years about December 13th

of Geneva. Nor does the incessant crackling of fir-cones in the Swiss forests bear any resemblance to the crackling sound heard by night on the glaciers.

In Majorca, the silence is deeper than anywhere else, though the asses and mules who spend the night at pasture interrupt it now and then by shaking their bells,[1] which have a less deep but more tuneful note than those carried by Swiss cows. So does the music of the *bolero* bursting out in the loneliest places and on the darkest nights. No peasant ever relinquishes his guitar, however late or early the hour. From my terrace I could hear the sea too, but so distant and so faint[2] that the fantastic and memorable poem of Djins came back to my mind:

J'écoute,
Tout fuit.
On doute
La nuit,
Tout passe,
L'espace
Efface
Le bruit.

I could hear a little child crying in a nearby farm. I could also hear his mother lulling him with a pretty native tune, very monotonous, very sad, very Arabic. But other, less poetic, voices came to remind me of Majorca's absurd side.

The hogs awoke and voiced their complaint in a mode that I am at a loss to define. Then the *pagés*, the paterfamilias, was roused by the voice of his beloved pigs, as the mother had been by the weeping of her baby. I heard him put his head out of the window and scold the inmates of the sty in authoritative tones. The pigs understood him perfectly, for they fell silent. Then the *pagés*, apparently with the hope of getting back to sleep, recited his rosary in a dismal voice which, according as drowsiness came and went, died away or rose again like the

[1] Sheep and goats now ring bells all night. Owls are also very vocal at this time of year; earlier, frogs and nightingales compete noisily.

[2] Her memory is at fault. If the weather had not yet broken, she could never have heard the surf from Palma, three miles away. The Mediterranean has no tides.

distant murmur of the waves. From time to time the hogs still let loose a wild cry; whereupon the peasant would raise his voice without interrupting his prayer, and the gentle beasts, calmed by an *Ora pro nobis* or an *Ave Maria* declaimed in a particular manner, grew quiet at once. As for the child, he was doubtless listening, eyes wide open, lost in the daze into which the nascent mind of cradled humanity, destined to perform mysterious labours within itself before signalizing its appearance, is plunged by unexplained noises.

Then our peace was interrupted by a sudden break in the weather. One early morning, after the long-drawn-out wailing of the wind had sung us lullabies all night, rain began beating on our windows, and we were awakened at last by the noise of the torrent which had begun to push its way through the stones of its dry bed. Next morning, its voice was louder; and on the third day, it was rolling along the boulders that obstructed its path. All the blossom had fallen from the trees, and streams of rainwater were coursing through the ill-protected rooms of our house.

The lack of precaution taken by Majorcans against these twin scourges of wind and rain is incomprehensible. Their delusion, or their bravado, is so remarkable that they flatly deny the existence of these adventitious, if serious, climatic variations. Until the very end of the two months of downpour which we were obliged to endure, they insisted that it never rained in Majorca.[1] Yet we also showed lack of foresight: a closer scrutiny of the mountain range and the direction of the prevailing winds would have made us realize the inevitable hardships that winter must entail.

[1] This trait is still remarkable; new seven-storey blocks of flats designed by the Palma Municipal Architect himself, have no chimneys, nor facilities for installing stoves, and therefore no adequate means of heating except electric fires, which only the very rich can afford to keep going. A similar denial that there is ever drought in summer may deprive the upper flats of water for several weeks on end; the pressure of the town water supply being too weak to serve them. Flat-dwellers huddle round charcoal braziers in the winter—the unseasoned wood used for the doors and windows lets in howling draughts and carries off the fumes—and in summer take buckets and borrow water from old-fashioned houses with rainwater wells. Only the best hotels are properly heated in winter.

But another trial lay in store for us: the one to which I refer above, when anticipating the end of my journey. A member of our family, who had a delicate constitution and was subject to a serious inflammation of the larynx, fell ill because of the damp. The House of the Wind (*Son Vent* in Mallorquin), as Señor Gomez called his villa, became uninhabitable; its walls being so thin that the lime with which our rooms were pargeted swelled up like a sponge. Never have I suffered so much from the cold, though the temperature was not really low: but people like us are used to keeping warm in winter, and this house had no fireplace. The damp settled like a cloak of ice over our shoulders, and reduced me to paralysis. We could not get used to the suffocating smell of the charcoal braziers,[1] and our invalid grew seriously ill and began to cough.

From this moment we became objects of horror to the people of Establiments. They tried and convicted us on a charge of pulmonary consumption which, in the prejudiced view of Spanish medicine, is as contagious and deadly as bubonic plague. A rich doctor who, for the modest fee of 45 francs, consented to pay us a visit, announced that it was nothing of consequence, and suggested no treatment. We had nicknamed him Dr. Marshmallow, on account of his single prescription. Another doctor was good enough to come to our help; but the shelves of the Palma pharmacies were so bare that we could obtain only the most disgusting drugs. Moreover, the illness seems to have been aggravated by causes which no science and no devotion could effectively combat. One morning, when we were greatly alarmed by the continuance of these rains and by the troubles directly and indirectly caused by them, a letter reached us from the boorish Gomez, announcing, in Spanish style, that we were harbouring a personage, who was harbouring a disease, which was bringing infection into his hearth, and constituted a threat

[1] The management of a charcoal brazier has to be learned. When first lighted it gives off strong carbon monoxide fumes which, if the charcoal has not been properly made, and the windows are closed, can even cause death. But a glowing heap of olive-pip charcoal, covered by a thin layer of ash and fed by pushing new fuel towards the centre from the sides, is healthy enough. I keep one in my study all winter and never let it go out between December and March

to the lives of his family; consequently he requested us to clear out of his palace with the least possible delay.

This caused me little regret, since I feared that if we stayed there much longer we should be drowned in our beds; but our invalid was in no condition to be moved, especially with the transport available, and in such weather too. Besides, the problem was where to go; for the news of our consumption had spread rapidly, and we could no longer hope to find any sort of lodging, even if we paid in gold and stayed for only a single night. We were well aware that whoever might offer to take us in would not be himself immune to prejudice, and that by accepting the favour we should involve him in the burden of censure which weighed upon us. But for the hospitality of the French consul, who worked miracles to gather us all under his roof, we should have faced the prospect of camping in some cave like proper gipsies.

Another miracle happened: we found a home for the winter. A Spanish political refugee of sorts had gone to earth in the deserted Carthusian monastery of Valldemosa. While visiting the Charterhouse—the poetry of which went to my head—we had been struck by his distinguished bearing, his wife's melancholy beauty, and the comfortable, if rustic, furnishings of their cell. It turned out that this enigmatical couple wanted to leave the country in haste, and that they were no less delighted to make over their cell to us, just as it stood, than we were to acquire it. Thus we came into possession of a completely furnished dwelling for the sum of a thousand francs; which was extremely reasonable (though in France we should not have had to pay more than a hundred crowns), so rare, costly and hard to assemble are the simplest essentials in Majorca.[1]

[1] On November 15th, Chopin had written from Son Vent to his friend Jules Fontana at Paris:

> Here I am in the midst of palms and cedars and cactuses and olives and lemons and aloes and figs and pomegranates. The sky is turquoise blue, the sea is azure, the mountains are emerald green; the air is as pure as that of Paradise. All day long the sun shines, and it is warm, and everybody wears summer clothes. At night one hears guitars and serenades.

He wrote again on December 3rd:

I have not been able to send you the manuscripts, since they are not ready. For the past three weeks I have been as sick as a dog, despite a heat of 18 degrees [Centigrade, equal to 63 Fahrenheit], despite the roses, orange trees, palms and flowering fig-trees. I caught a bad cold. The three most celebrated doctors of the island met for a consultation. One peered at what I had expectorated, the second sounded the organs of expectoration, the third listened while I expectorated again. The first said that I would die, the second that I was dying, the third that I was already dead. And yet I live as I used to live in the past. I cannot pardon Jeannot for failing to give me any advice on the treatment of the acute bronchitis from which he must have been perfectly aware that I suffered. I had great difficulty in escaping leeches, cuppings and similar operations. Thank God I am now myself again. But my illness interfered with my *Preludes*, which you will receive God knows when.

After a few days I shall be living in the loveliest spot on earth: sea, mountains . all one could wish. We are going to live in an old, ruined, abandoned Carthusian monastery, from which Mendizábal seems to have expelled the monks expressly for my sake. It is quite near Palma and nothing could be more charming: cells, a most poetic cemetery . in fact, I am convinced that I shall feel well there. The one thing I still lack is my piano. I have written to Pleyel. Ask him about it and say that I fell ill the day after I arrived here, but that I am getting better. Say little, generally, about my manuscripts. Write to me. So far I haven't had a single letter from you.

Tell Leo that I haven't yet sent the *Preludes* to Albrecht, but that I love them well and will write soon. Post the enclosed letter to my parents yourself, and write as soon as possible. Greetings to Jeannot. Tell nobody that I have been ill; it could only encourage gossip.

Your Chopin.

According to George Sand, the weather broke about December 7th; Chopin then fell a victim to the damp, and after a miserable experience with draughts, braziers and doctors, they were evicted by Gomez. But according to this letter, his illness was caused by a cold caught on his arrival at Palma, during a spell of unusual heat, which lasted until December 3rd —when the decision to move to Valldemosa had already been taken.

The truth probably is that a heavy storm towards the end of November made them realize that Son Vent, being built as a summer house, would become impossibly cold and draughty by Christmas. So having already come to an agreement with Ignacio Durán, the tenant of the Carthusian cell, George vacated Son Vent before the new month began and planted her family on M. Fleury, the French Consul at Palma, for four days. There Chopin consulted the three doctors, who correctly diagnosed consumption. Gomez, who had expected a lease for the whole winter, was naturally vexed when she came to his town house and handed back the key. Then one of the doctors talked indiscreetly about Chopin's symptoms; Gomez's vexation turned to alarm and he considered himself entitled to damages. Majorcans still burn the bedding on which a consumptive has lain, fumigate the house and rub the bedstead with vinegar.

Since we now spent four days in Palma—meanwhile the deluge continued and I rarely left the fireplace which the Consul had the good fortune to possess—I shall here interrupt my narrative with a short description of the island's capital. Let me present M. Laurens, who came in the following year to explore and sketch its finest aspects, as the reader's guide; he is a far better archæologist than I am.

Chapter Eight

ALTHOUGH Majorca was occupied for four hundred years by the Moors, few relics of them survive. Their only architectural remains in Palma consist of a small Baths.[1] No Roman remains at all, and the Carthaginians have left a few ruins near Alcudia, their ancient capital,[2] and the tradition of Hannibal's birth, which M. Grasset ascribes to the overweening conceit of the Majorcans, although the tale is not entirely improbable. 'They claim that Hamilcar, on the way from Africa to Catalonia with his wife, who was then pregnant, visited a Majorcan headland crowned by a temple of Lucina, Goddess of Childbirth, and that Hannibal was born there. The same account is to be found in the *History of Majorca* by Dameto.'[3]

Yet Moorish taste survives in the smallest structural details, and M. Laurens has had to correct the archæological errors of his predecessors, lest uninformed travellers like myself should believe they were discovering genuine traces of Arab architecture at every step.

'I saw no houses in Palma,' writes M. Laurens, 'which seemed very ancient. All those most interesting as regards architecture

[1] By no means the only ones. The *Almudaina*, or Royal Palace of the Moorish Kings, though rebuilt as a Christian Royal Palace, dates from the twelfth century. A Moorish gateway spans the Calle de la Almudaina. The Church of San Miguel began as a mosque.

[2] Majorca was never held by the Carthaginians in strength. They found Minorca (Port Mahon is called after their general Mago) and Iviza more easily controlled. The Alcudia ruins are Graeco-Roman; Alcudia seems to have been the Latin *Cunici*. North African Vandals are said to have destroyed the Roman cities in the fifth century A.D.; but they preserved a Roman aqueduct near Pollensa and did not desecrate the Roman graves.

[3] El Torre, an islet near Palma, was known as 'The Islet of Hannibal' (Pliny: *Natural History* iii. 11). The island of Formentera is said to have belonged to Hannibal's father Hamilcar.

and antiquity dated from the beginning of the sixteenth century, but here the elegant and brilliant art of that period had a different fruition than in France. These houses boast only two storeys, and a low attic.' (I should myself prefer to call them drying-rooms, rather than attics; the country word is '*porchos*'.) 'The street entrance consists of an unornamented arch; its size, however, and the large number of dressed stones radiating outwards from it are most imposing. Tall windows divided by exaggeratedly slender pillars light the spacious rooms of the ground floor and lend them a thoroughly Arab look.[1] So strong is this characteristic, that I visited more than twenty houses built on the same model, investigating every detail of their structure, before I convinced myself that these windows had not been spoil filched from the walls of those fairy-like Moorish palaces, of which the Alhambra at Granada is a surviving example. Nowhere but in Majorca have I found six-foot pillars with a diameter of only three inches. The fine quality of their marble,[2] and the style of the surmounting capital had all led me to assume an Arab source. Be that as it may, these windows are as beautiful as original. The attic is a gallery, with closely-set openings imitating those which crown the *Lonja*, or Exchange.[3] A projecting roof, supported by skilfully carved beams, guards this floor against rain or sun, making effective patterns of light and shade by the long shadows it casts on the house, and by the contrast between the brownish block of the masonry and the bright tints of the sky. A grandly-conceived staircase leads up from a central courtyard, but between this and the street entrance a vestibule intervenes, remarkable for the capitals of its pilasters, which are ornamented either with carved foliage or with an escutcheon supported by angels.

'For more than a century after the Renaissance, the Majorcans continued to build extremely luxurious private houses.[4] While

[1] Since the Moors and their former Jewish subjects who remained in Palma after the Conquest outnumbered the Christians, an eastern style persisted except in Ecclesiastical architecture.

[2] Santañy stone. [3] He is referring to the pierced balustrade of the Lonja

[4] One of the most splendid, the Casa Berga in the Plaza Catalina Tomás, is today being gutted to make room for municipal offices. Another, in the Calle Morey, has become an engineering workshop.

retaining the same general architectural plan, they adapted current Continental fashions to their vestibules and staircases. Hence the frequent intrusion of the Tuscan or Doric column; and the design of the ramps and balustrades lends an opulent look to every aristocratic mansion. This fondness for lavish ornamental staircases and for the Arab style is evinced in the poorest houses, even when one single steep flight of steps leads straight from the street to the first floor; for each step is faced with earthenware tiles florally decorated in blue, yellow or red.'

M. Laurens's description is accurate, and his drawings successfully reproduce the elegance of these interiors, whose peristyles would provide us with admirably simple theatre sets.

Sometimes the small paved *patios* are surrounded by columns resembling the *cortile* of a Venetian palace; most of them also have a chastely designed well in the centre, and they neither look like, nor serve the same purpose as, our own bare, dirty courtyards. They never give access to stables and coach-houses but are genuine inner courts, perhaps harking back to the Roman *atrium*. The central well obviously derives from the *impluvium*.

When these peristyles are decorated with pots of flowers and shrubs, their grace and severity combine in a poetic charm that is quite lost on the Majorcan nobility, since they seldom fail to apologize for the antiquity of their homes. If you admire the architecture, they smile, passing your praise off as a joke and perhaps secretly despising such extravagant French politeness. Moreover, not everything is so poetic in these mansions as their entrances. I should be greatly embarrassed to describe certain unhygienic details to my readers unless I could do so in Latin, like Jacquemont when he is discussing Indian customs. But since I am no Latinist, I must refer those who are interested to the passage which M. Grasset, a less responsible writer than M. Laurens, but perfectly truthful on this point, devotes to the condition of larders found in Majorca, as well as in the old houses of Spain and Italy. It is well worth reading, if only for his quotation of a quaint Spanish medical prescription still popular in Majorca.[1]

The insides of these palaces, in fact, by no means correspond

[1] Grasset de Saint Sauveur, p. 119.

Dancing to castanets. A sketch by Maurice Sand

Products of the pig. From a water-colour by G. Trajani

The Christmas lottery at Palma. From a water-colour by G. Trajani

to the outsides. There is nothing more revealing than the arrangement and furnishing of the home, whether one is considering the question nationally or individually. In Paris, where the whims of fashion and the abundance of manufactured goods permit a remarkable variety of interior effects, one need only enter a well-to-do person's house to form a quick judgement of his character. It will be plain at a glance whether he has taste or method, greed or carelessness, a tidy mind or a romantic one, hospitality or ostentation. Like most people, I have my own system for judging in this way; and frequently, I confess, draw false conclusions. Especially detestable to me is an under-furnished and scrupulously tidy room. Unless the occupant happens to possess great intelligence and a nobility of heart that transcends the sphere of such unimportant material considerations, and allows him to treat his home as a mere tabernacle, I diagnose an empty head and a cold heart. I cannot understand people who, while living between four walls, feel no need to furnish these, if only with logs and baskets, and to have something alive around them, though it were nothing better than a miserable potted pink, or a bedraggled sparrow.

Emptiness and stillness terrify me, symmetry and strict order overwhelm me with gloom; and if I could accept the idea of eternal damnation, my Hell would certainly be to live eternally in one of those provincial houses ruled by meticulous order, where nothing is ever moved or left lying about, where nothing is ever worn out or broken, and where no animal is admitted, on the principle that animate things damage the inanimate. You may burn all the carpets in the world, if I may enjoy them only on condition of never seeing a child, a cat or dog frisking over them! Such impeccability does not derive from a true love of cleanliness, but either from extreme indolence or from a mean and sordid nature. With reasonable care, the housekeeper of my choice could see that our home remained in the active state of cleanliness which I find indispensable to comfort. But what of a family that cannot offer cleanliness as either an excuse or a pretext for an empty and static home?

Though one may easily be mistaken, as I have just said, when drawing conclusions from individual instances, one is rarely mistaken in general cases. A people's character stands revealed by their domestic customs and furnishings, as clearly as by their features and language. Having scoured Palma in search of rooms, I visited a fair number of houses. The contents of all were so remarkably alike that I could deduce from them a character common to the inhabitants. Nowhere did my heart fail to be wrung with distress and boredom at the mere sight of such bare walls, such stained and grubby flagstones, such scant and dirty furniture. Everything cried out in witness against carelessness and indolence; there was never a book to be seen, never a piece of handiwork. The men did not read, the women did not even sew.[1] A smell of garlic from the kitchen was the only indication of domestic activity; and the only signs of private recreation were cigar butts littering the floor.[2]

This lack of intellectual energy gives a house a lifelessness and emptiness unparalleled in France, and makes the Majorcans seem more like Africans than Europeans. All these mansions where generation has followed generation without making the least change in their surroundings, or leaving any individual impression on things which are, to some extent, part of ordinary human life, suggest caravanserais rather than private houses; and while our French homes resemble family nests, theirs resemble shelters where bands of nomads seek a random night's lodging. Well-informed travellers tell me that this comment holds good for the whole of Spain.

To recapitulate: the peristyle, or *atrium*, of mansions owned by the *Cavallers* (as the nobility of Majorca still style themselves) has a great air of welcome and even of comfort. But after climbing the elegant staircase and penetrating into the house itself, you might be in a building dedicated solely to the *siesta*. Enormous rooms, usually rectangular in shape, very lofty, very cool,

[1] Probably she means the ladies of the Cavaller families. Majorcan women in general were famous for their embroidery at this time and certainly did their own dressmaking.

[2] Balzac wrote about George Sand's drawing-room at 16 Rue Pigalle, Paris, a couple of years later: 'The drawing-room where she receives is full of superb Chinese vases filled with flowers. The furniture is green, there is a cabinet filled with curios, pictures by Delacroix, her portrait by Calamatta. The piano is magnificent. Chopin is always about. She smokes cigarettes and nothing else. . . .'

very dark, entirely bare, ascetically whitewashed and decorated only with enormous age-blackened family portraits, hung in a single row so high up that the subjects cannot be distinguished; four or five chairs, seated and backed in worm-eaten cowhide, secured to the solid frame with great gilded studs which have not been cleaned for two hundred years; one or two Valencian mats,[1] or long-haired sheepskins thrown at random on the paving; casement windows set very high up and heavily curtained; wide doors of the same dark oak as is used in the raftered ceiling, and sometimes an antique door-curtain of gold brocade richly embroidered with the family coat of arms, but tarnished and mildewed by age; this is what Majorcan palaces look like inside. You hardly ever see any tables except dining tables; mirrors are most uncommon, and occupy so small an area of the huge frames which enclose them, that they cast no light worth mentioning.

The master of the house will be found on his feet, smoking amid a deep silence, the mistress will be occupying a huge chair and flirting her fan without a thought in her head. No children are ever to be seen: they live with the servants in the kitchen, or the attic, or somewhere else; the parents do not bother about them. A chaplain wanders idly around the house. The twenty or thirty menservants take their siesta, while a hirsute chambermaid opens the door at the visitor's fifteenth ring of the bell. This sort of life is certainly not lacking in *character*, as we would say nowadays, making the word mean almost anything, or nothing; but if even the most placid middle-class Frenchman were condemned to endure it, I am sure that either despair or spiritual reaction would soon make a demagogue of him.

[1] Made in Palma. One mat-making house, Ca' La Seu, claims to have been founded in the fifteenth century by the ancestors of its present owners.

Chapter Nine

THE three most important edifices in Palma are the Cathedral, the Lonja (or Exchange), and the Royal Palace. The building of the Cathedral, with which the Majorcans credit King James the Conqueror, their first Christian king and as it were their Charlemagne, was indeed begun in his reign, though not finished until 1601. This huge, majestic pile, which stands on the seashore, greatly impresses the visitor as he enters the harbour; but though the limestone used throughout is of a very fine texture and a lovely amber in colour, he finds nothing there of real stylistic value, except the southern portal, which M. Laurens describes as the finest specimen of Gothic art that he had ever had the opportunity of drawing. The interior is extremely austere and dark.

Because sea winds screamed through the wide chinks of the main door and rattled the pictures and the consecrated vessels during services, the doors and rose-windows facing the harbour have now been bricked up. The nave measures no less than five hundred and forty palms in length, and three hundred and seventy-five in width.[1] In the centre of the chancel stands a very simple marble sarcophagus, which the guide opens to show visitors the mummified corpse of James II, son of the Conqueror: a pious prince, as weak and gentle as his father was venturesome and warlike.[2]

The Majorcans insist that their Cathedral is greatly superior to that of Barcelona—a claim which cannot be substantiated[3]—just

[1] Five palms make a metre.

[2] Now decently kept in the Chapel of the Holy Trinity.

[3] I find it nobler, loftier, better proportioned, and far less cluttered.

as their Exchange is said to be infinitely more beautiful than that of Valencia—which it may be, for all I know, since I have never been to Valencia. Both Cathedral organs display the curious trophy characteristic of Spanish provincial capitals: a hideous turbaned Moor's head in painted wood, forming the end of the pendentive. Such severed heads are often embellished with long white beards, and splashed with red paint below to show how tainted was the blood of the conquered.[1] On the keystones of the aisle arches many coats of arms are emblazoned. Thus to blazon one's armorial bearings in the House of God was a privilege for which the Majorcan Cavallers paid exorbitant fees; and it was thanks to this vanity-tax that the Cathedral could be completed in a century when Catholic devotion had somewhat cooled. Yet it would be unfair to ascribe to the Majorcans alone a weakness which they shared at that epoch with the religious aristocracy of the whole world.

Of all these buildings the one which impressed me most deeply was the Exchange; the originality of its conception has not precluded a faultless and simple symmetry. It was begun and finished during the first half of the fifteenth century. The famous Jovellanos described it in detail, and the *Magazin Pittoresque* popularized it several years ago with a drawing of great interest. It consists of one enormous room supported by six slender, graceful, spirally fluted columns. Intended in the old days as a meeting place for the many merchants and sailors who flocked to Palma, the Exchange now attests the lost splendours of Majorcan trade, being reserved for public festivals.[2] We should have been interested to see the Majorcans, clad in the sumptuous costumes of their ancestors, disporting themselves solemnly in this ancient ballroom; but the spectacle took place when rain held us prisoners on the mountain and prevented us from watching their carnival, which is both less famous and, I gather, less gloomy than that of Venice. Nevertheless, the Exchange, lovely though I thought it, cannot rival in my memory

[1] There has never been such a head in Palma Cathedral.

[2] So internationally famous was it in 1460 that the Genoese Exchange became redundant and the King of Aragon converted it into a church. The Palma *Lonja* is now a museum; but the exhibits are few and undistinguished.

that charming jewel on the Grand Canal called the Cadoro by the Venetians.

The Royal Palace of Palma, which M. Grasset does not hesitate to describe as Romanesque and Moorish (this aroused in him feelings entirely appropriate to the taste of the First Empire), is said to have been built in 1309. M. Laurens declares that his conscience was disturbed by the little twin windows, and the mysterious colonettes which he examined here. Would it then be too bold to ascribe the anomalies of style that characterize so many Majorcan edifices to the inclusion of old fragments in later buildings? Just as, in France and Italy, Renaissance artists incorporated genuine Greek and Roman medallions and bas-reliefs in sculptural decoration, may not the Majorcan Christians, after tearing down all Moorish monuments, have increasingly made use of those rich ruins for the adornment of their own?

The capture and sack of Palma by the Christians, on the last day of the year 1229, are vividly described in the *Chronicle of Marsigli* (hitherto unpublished). I quote a fragment:

> The plunderers who ransacked the houses found in them the most beautiful Moorish women and girls, with their laps full of gold and silver coins, pearls and precious stones, gold and silver bracelets, sapphires and every kind of costly jewel. They displayed all these things to the armed men who appeared before them and, weeping bitterly, said in Saracen: 'All these are yours; leave only enough to provide us with food.'
>
> Such was the lust for gain, such the dissolution of discipline, that the men of the royal household of Aragon, engrossed in the search for hidden valuables, did not appear before the King for an entire week. It had come to such a pass that, since neither the cook nor any other royal servitor could be found, one Ladro, an Aragonese nobleman, said to King James: 'My Lord, I invite you to be my guest, for I have plenty to eat, and it appears that I have a fine cow in my quarters; there you may eat and sleep tonight.'
>
> The King was delighted, and followed the said nobleman.

Nothing could be more picturesque than the appearance of the Royal Palace, which is unsymmetrical, inconvenient, uncivilized and mediæval; yet at the same time nothing could be prouder, more individual and more *hidalgoish* than this seignorial manor composed of galleries, towers, terraces and archways, climbing up on one another's shoulders to a considerable height, and culminating in a Gothic angel[1] who, from the bosom of the clouds, gazes across the sea to Spain.

This Palace, where the archives of the island are stored, is the residence of the Captain-General, the most important person in Majorca.[2]

M. Grasset describes the interior as follows:

'One first enters a hall used as a guard house. On the right of this lie two large apartments, where there is hardly a chair to be found. The third room, the audience-chamber, contains a decorative crimson velvet throne fringed with gold and placed on a carpeted dais three steps high. At either side stands a lion of gilded wood. The canopy over the throne is made of the same crimson velvet and crowned by ostrich plumes. Above the throne hang the portraits of the King and Queen. Here the Captain-General receives, on ceremonial occasions or gala days, representatives of the various branches of the civil administration, the garrison officers, and important foreign visitors.'

The Captain-General, who acted as Governor, and to whom we had letters of introduction, did indeed honour us by receiving in the audience-chamber one[3] who undertook to present them to him. Our envoy found this exalted functionary near his throne, which must have been the very one described by M. Grasset in 1807; because it was worn, faded, threadbare, and stained with oil and candle-grease. Though the wooden lions had lost most of their gilt, they still wore a very savage

[1] Cast by Campredon, a metal-worker of the early fourteenth century, and still in position, though struck by lightning in 1431 and later damaged by the fireworks which celebrated the victory of Lepanto. It acts as a weathercock, and the Majorcans describe an unstable man as being 'like the Palace Angel'.

[2] When a war is in progress, the Captain-General becomes the most important. In peacetime he defers to the Civil Governor.

[3] Chopin.

expression. Only the royal effigy had changed; this time it was not Ferdinand VII, but the chaste Isabella[1] who, like a colossal inn-sign, filled the ancient gilt frame where her august ancestors had succeeded one another, like models in an art-school frame. The Governor, though housed like Hoffman's Duqué d'Irénéus, was none the less a man of high repute and princely graciousness.

A fourth very interesting building is the Palace of the Palma City Fathers, dating from the sixteenth century. Its roof is remarkable for the projecting eaves, which somewhat resemble those of Florentine palaces or Swiss chalets; and it has also the unusual feature of being supported by wooden caissons, richly carved with rosettes and alternating with tall caryatids stretched out beneath the eaves, which they seem to bear up sorrowfully, for most of them have their faces buried in their hands.[2]

I have not been inside this building, which contains a portrait gallery of Majorcan celebrities. Among these distinguished people the renowned King James of Aragon is seen, portrayed as *King of Diamonds*. An ancient painting shows the funeral of the enlightened Majorcan scholar Ramon Llull;[3] and a most varied array of ancient costumes worn by people in the procession. Finally there is a splendid St. Sebastian by Van Dyck, to the existence of which no one in Majorca thought fit to draw my attention.

'Palma boasts an art-school,' M. Laurens continues. 'In this century alone it has produced thirty-six painters, eight sculptors, eleven architects and six engravers, all of them—if we may trust the *Dictionary of Famous Majorcan Artists*, just published by the learned Don Antonio Furió—famous practitioners.' I must

1 She had reputedly taken a bull-fighter for a lover.

2 These caryatids, who alternate with bearded men naked except for floral girdles, must have covered their faces when George Sand passed; they have gazed frankly down ever since.

3 A wild young nobleman in the train of King James, who had a sudden change of heart when a married woman, whom he pursued into a church, uncovered her breast and revealed a frightful cancer. Llull became the greatest mystical poet of the thirteenth century, and one of its leading philosophers. Martyred in old age while trying to convert the Moors, he is now the Blessed Ramon Llull, but has never been canonized, because in order to win over the Moors he spoke too respectfully of the Koran. The Majorcans for centuries have been pressing his claim to sainthood.

ingenuously confess that during my stay in Palma I never realized that I was surrounded by so many great men, nor saw anything that led me to guess their existence. . . .[1] One or two wealthy families own paintings of the Spanish School. . . . However, if you look round the shops, if you visit the houses of the ordinary citizen, you will find nothing but coloured prints of the sort that pedlars display in the market places of France, and that there find a home only under the peasant's lowly roof.

Palma's greatest pride is the Palace of the Count of Montenegro, now an old man in his eighties, formerly Captain-General, by birth one of the most illustrious, and in wealth one of the leading, figures of Majorca. He owns a library which we were permitted to inspect; but I did not open a single book there, and should be unable to give even the vaguest description of it (so closely akin to terror is my reverence for books) had not a learned compatriot of mine informed me how important were the treasures before which I had heedlessly passed, like the cock in the fable that disregarded the pearls. This Frenchman, M. Tastu, an erudite linguist, and married to one of our most talented and noble-souled Muses, had spent nearly two years in Catalonia and Majorca on a study of Romance languages. He kindly lent me his notes, and authorized me, with a generosity very rare among scholars, to make whatever use of them I liked. I shall not do so without warning my reader that this traveller was as enthusiastic about all things Majorcan as I had been unenthusiastic.

To explain this difference of impressions I could plead that, throughout my stay, the Majorcans were herded uncomfortably close together to make room for twenty thousand Spanish war-refugees from the mainland: thus it may not have been due to mistake or prejudice that I found Palma less habitable, and the Majorcans less ready to welcome a fresh complement of foreigners, than doubtless had been the case two years before. But it is better to incur the censure of some kindly-disposed person who will correct me, than describe things in any light

[1] The Beaux-Arts Club is one of the most honoured institutions in Palma, which boasts more painters and more art-galleries than any other Spanish city, except perhaps Madrid and Barcelona.

except that in which I saw them myself. Moreover, I shall welcome a public refutation and rebuke, in addition to what I have been privately accorded, in the form of a more accurate and interesting book on Majorca than this disconnected and perhaps, after all, biased account.

So let M. Tastu publish the account of his journey; I shall read with the most heartfelt pleasure, I swear, anything that may make me change my mind about the Majorcans. I have known a few of them whom I should like to consider representative types and who, I hope, will never doubt the warmth of my feelings for them, should this book ever fall into their hands.

I find, then, in M. Tastu's notes on the intellectual riches of Majorca, a mention of this library, which I went through so casually in the wake of the Count of Montenegro's private Chaplain; being far more interested in the domestic details of this old bachelor Cavaller's home. A sad and sober home, if ever there was one, governed by a silent priest.

'This library,' M. Tastu writes, 'was formed by the present Count's uncle, Cardinal Antonio Despuig, a close friend of Pope Pius VI. The learned Cardinal collected everything of bibliographical interest to be found in Spain, Italy and France; the section dealing with numismatology and ancient art is especially comprehensive. Among the small number of manuscripts it contains, is one of great interest to students of calligraphy: a Book of Hours with exquisite miniatures, belonging to the best period of mediæval art. Visitors instructed in heraldry will find there an Armorial showing Spanish coats of arms correctly blazoned, including those of noble families from Aragon, Majorca, Roussillon and Languedoc. The manuscript, which seems to date from the sixteenth century, belonged to the Dameto family, who are connected with the Despuigs and the Montenegros. Glancing through it, we found the coat of arms of the Bonaparts, the ancestors of our great Napoleon.

'Another treasure still to be found in this library is the lovely chart made in 1439 by the Majorcan Valseca:[1] a masterpiece of

[1] Majorca was famous for its cartography until the eighteenth century. A beautiful fifteenth-century map of the world by an unknown Majorcan is preserved in the Palace of the Parelladas at Palma.

penmanship and topography, enriched by the precious labour of the miniaturist. It was once owned by Amerigo Vespucci, who had bought it for a remarkably high price, as is evidenced by a contemporary inscription on the back: *Questa ampla pelle di geographia fù pagata da Amerigo Vespucci CXXX ducati di oro di marco.* This valuable example of mediæval geography will soon be published as a supplement to the Catalano-Majorcan Atlas of 1375 [*Manuscripts noted by the Academy of Inscriptions and Belles Lettres, Vol. XIV, Part 2.*]'

As I copy the above passage, my scalp crawls at a dreadful recollection. We were in this Library, and the Chaplain was unrolling this very chart for us to admire—this unique treasure for which Amerigo Vespucci paid 130 gold ducats more than four hundred years ago, and for which the antiquarian Cardinal Despuig paid Heaven knows how much. . . . One of the Count's forty or fifty servants had the bright idea of placing an inkstand on one of the corners of the parchment to keep it spread open on the table. The inkstand, which was made of cork, had been filled to the brim!

Suddenly the parchment, used to being rolled up, and maybe inspired by some evil spirit, gave a heave, a crackle, and a bound, and before anyone could restrain it, triumphantly curled up on itself, inkstand and all. A general cry of horror rose; the Chaplain turned paler even than the parchment. They unrolled the map slowly, still cherishing the idle hope that no damage had been done. Alas! The inkstand was empty. The map was flooded, and the pretty little kings painted in miniature were literally sailing on a sea blacker than the Euxine.

Everyone panicked. I believe that the Chaplain fainted away. The servants rushed up with buckets of water, as if a fire had broken out, and began vigorously cleaning the map with sponges and scrubbing brushes. Before we could restrain their fatal zeal, kings, seas, islands and continents were sent packing, helter-skelter. The map was not, however, irremediably spoiled: M. Tastu had made an accurate tracing of it, and thanks to him, the damage will be to some extent reparable. But what must have been the Chaplain's dismay when his master learned of the accident! Though we were all standing six feet from the table at the time, I am certain that the whole weight of blame was none the less placed on our shoulders, and that this has not helped to restore French prestige in Majorca.[1] Hence we were disinclined to admire or even notice any of the other wonders in the Palace: the collection of medals, the antique bronzes, the paintings. We were anxious only to escape before the Count returned; and, convinced that we should be made the scapegoats, dared not revisit the scene of the disaster. M. Tastu must therefore once more be cited to correct my ignorance:

'Adjoining the Cardinal's library is a priceless collection of Celtiberian, Moorish, Greek, Roman and mediæval medals; now in a lamentable state of chaos and waiting for a scholar to arrange and classify it. The Count of Montenegro's rooms are decorated with antique marbles and bronzes, either excavated at Aricia, or bought in Rome by the Cardinal. He also owns many Spanish and Italian pictures, several of which would not disgrace the finest galleries of Europe.'[2]

I must also mention Belver, or Bellver, Castle, built as a residence for the Majorcan Kings, majestically commanding the sea from its hill about a mile to the south of Palma. This is a very ancient fortress, and one of the harshest state prisons in Spain. 'Its well-preserved walls,' writes M. Laurens, 'were raised at the close of the thirteenth century, and make it one of the most interesting mediæval fortresses extant.' When he visited the Castle, as I did not, he came across some fifty naked Carlist prisoners, many of them only children, who with boisterous high spirits were filling their mess-tins from a cauldron of coarse, boiled macaroni. Their guards sat smoking cigars as they knitted stockings.

It was, in fact, to Belver Castle, that the overflow from the Barcelona prisons had been diverted. But these formidable doors have closed on still more celebrated prisoners. Here Don Gaspar de Jovellanos, one of the most gifted orators and the most forceful writers of Spain, paid the penalty for his famous pamphlet

[1] She panicked unnecessarily. Only a small stain was left.

[2] The Montenegro treasures were finally dispersed about fifty years ago; later I bought a few of the less important pictures and some of the china from a dealer.

Bread and Bulls. He was incarcerated in the dungeon of the 'Tower of Homage,' writes Vargas, 'which is the most brutal of prisons.'[1] Jovellanos occupied his dreary leisure by composing a scholarly description of the Castle, in which he recalled the many tragic scenes that it had witnessed during the wars of the Middle Ages. The Majorcans are also indebted to his enforced stay in their island for an admirable description of the Cathedral and Exchange. His *Letters on Majorca* are, in fact, the most reliable historic sources available.

[1] 'Dungeon' suggests a damp basement room, on a level with the moat. Jovellanos was not punished for this pamphlet. Nor was he confined in the Tower of Homage, but occupied a room on the second storey with a wide view of the hills and next door to the Castle kitchen. He has left a short poem scratched on the wall, protesting that his only crime was his innocence.

Chapter Ten

THE dungeon to which the parasite vicars of the Prince of Peace consigned Jovellanos presently housed another scientific and political celebrity: a man as deservedly famous in France as Jovellanos is in Spain. His little-known story will interest my readers as one more romantic chapter in a life which scientific ardour condemned to a thousand hazardous and moving adventures.

In 1808 M. Arago, whom Napoleon had commissioned to measure the meridian, was working in Majorca when news reached the island of the events at Madrid and the abduction of King Ferdinand.[1] So infuriated were the Majorcans that they set out in a crowd for the mountain called the Clot de Galatzo,[2] where M. Arago was taking observations, to wreak vengeance on him for being a Frenchman. The mountain rises above the coast where James of Aragon first landed before conquering Majorca from the Moors in 1229; and since M. Arago often used to light fires up there for warmth, they decided that he must be signalling a French squadron, which stood by, to send a landing-force ashore. However, a Majorcan named Damian, who was quartermaster of the Spanish naval brig detailed to assist M. Arago in his task, resolved to warn him of the danger by which he was threatened. Running ahead of

[1] Napoleon had been in supposed alliance with Spain. The combined French and Spanish fleets were first defeated at Cape St. Vincent, then destroyed at Trafalgar. To keep the Spaniards in line, Napoleon invaded Spain, summoned King Charles IV to an interview at Bayonne, forced him to abdicate; did the same with Charles's successor Ferdinand VII, and then conferred the throne on his own brother, Joseph Bonaparte.

[2] A mistake. *Clot* means valley, or cavity, or a fold in the hills, not the hill itself.

his fellow-countrymen, Damian reached the observation-hut in time to disguise him as a sailor. M. Arago at once left the mountain and made for Palma. On the way he met the excited crowd of patriots who asked him whether he had seen the accursed *gabacho*,[1] whom they proposed to tear limb from limb. Having learned to speak Mallorquin fluently, however, he answered their questions without being recognized.

At Palma he went aboard the brig; but Captain Don Manuel de Vacaro, who had hitherto punctiliously obeyed M. Arago's orders, would not take him to Barcelona, and the only refuge he offered on board was a crate which proved too small to accommodate M. Arago. Next day, a threatening mob gathered on the quay and Captain Vacaro warned him that he could no longer answer for his life; adding, on the advice of the Captain-General, that his one hope of safety lay in surrender to the Constable of Bellver Castle. M. Arago, who agreed, was provided with a launch in which he crossed the harbour; but the mob gave chase, and were hard at his heels when the gates of the fortress closed on him. Here he spent two months until at last the Captain-General notified him that he would turn a blind eye to his escape, which he made good with the help of M. Rodriguez, his Spanish scientific colleague. The same Damian, who had saved his life at the Clot de Galatzo, took him to Algiers by fishing boat but would not, for any price, land him either in France or in Spain. During his imprisonment, M. Arago had been told by his Swiss guards[2] that certain monks of the island had unsuccessfully bribed them to poison him. In Algiers he met with many other setbacks, from which he was even luckier to escape; but these would be irrelevant to our theme, though we hope that one day he will publish his story.

The character of Palma is not immediately revealed to the casual visitor. But if he takes a stroll at dusk through its deep mysterious streets, he will be impressed by the graceful style and original placing of even its less distinguished buildings. And

[1] Frenchman: from the name of a French-Pyrenean people.

[2] This is facetious. Swiss guards were celebrated for their discipline and pomp. M. Arago means: 'the raggle-taggle Majorcan militia.'

if he approaches Palma from the fields to the north, its African aspect is most challenging.

This romantic beauty would not have struck the ordinary archæologist as it did M. Laurens. He has described one of the views which, as it happens, had made the deepest impression on me by its majestic melancholy: a stretch of the city walls, not far from the church of San Agustin, where rises a huge square block, with no other opening than a little arched door, crowned by a clump of beautiful palm-trees. This is all that remains of a Templar fortress, and makes a fine, sorrowful, arid foreground for the splendid picture which unfolds beyond: the smiling, fruitful plain bounded in the distance by the blue mountains of Valldemosa. Towards evening the colour of the landscape changes hourly, growing ever more and more harmonious; at sunset we have watched it change from glistening pink, to magnificent purple, then to silvery mauve, finally at the onset of night to pure, transparent blue.

M. Laurens has sketched several other views taken from the walls of Palma. 'Every evening,' he writes, 'at the hour when the sun colours things most vividly, I used to stroll along the ramparts, pausing at every turn to observe the chance felicities produced by the relations between the outlines of the mountains, or the sea, and the tops of the city buildings. The embankment on this side of the ramparts was fledged with a terrifying aloe hedge, from which sprang hundreds of those tall, flowering stalks like huge branched candelabra. Beyond, clumps of palm-trees grew in the gardens, surrounded by fig-trees, cacti, orange-trees and castor-oil plants as large as trees; farther off rose belvederes and vine-shaded terraces; farther still, the Cathedral spires and the towers and domes of the many churches stood silhouetted against the clear bright background of the sky.'

Another walk in which M. Laurens's preferences coincided with mine was among the ruins of the Dominican Monastery. At the end of a vine arbour supported by marble columns were four tall palm-trees, giganticized by the elevation of their terrace-garden and from this vantage point forming an integral part of the buildings with which their crests are level. Through their

San Nicolás Church and Casa Berga, Palma, 1838.
A sketch by Maurice Sand

Valldemosan peasants. A sketch by Maurice Sand

An evening party at Maria Antonia's. A sketch by Maurice Sand

Maurice and Solange eating too many oranges. A sketch by Maurice Sand

branches one glimpsed the top of the facade of St. Etienne, the great solid tower[1] in which the famous Balearic clock is set, and the Angel Tower of the Royal Palace. The Balearic Clock, by the way, which has been described at length by the two chief historians of Majorca, Dameto and Mut, was still working thirty years ago, and here is what M. Grasset says of it in his *Journey to the Balearic and Pityusian Isles* (1807):

> This very ancient piece of machinery is called the Sun Clock. It marks the hours from sunrise to sunset, following the greater or lesser extension of the diurnal and nocturnal course; with the result that, on the 10th of June, it strikes the first hour of the day at half-past five, and the fourteenth at half-past seven, the first of the night at half-past eight, the ninth at half-past four next morning. Beginning with December 10th, the process is reversed. From year's end to year's end the hours are accurately regulated by the variations between sunrise and sunset. Though of no great use to the Majorcans, who tell the time by more modern clocks, this contraption serves to remind the gardeners of their watering-hours. Nobody knows from where and at what date it was brought to Majorca; presumably it did not come from Spain, France, Germany or Italy, where the Romans had introduced the practice of dividing the day into twelve hours, beginning with sunrise. However, an ecclesiastic, the Rector of Palma University, declares, in the third part of his work on the Seraphic [Sephardic?] religion that, under Vespasian, Jewish refugees rescued this celebrated clock from the ruins of Jerusalem and carried it to Majorca, where they fled for safety. There you have a wonderful origin, in keeping with the characteristic partiality of our islanders for everything that smacks of the sensational. The historian Dameto, and Mut, who resumes the story where Dameto lays down his pen, trace the

[1] This Monastery with its gardens extended up the slope from what is now the Teatro Lirico to the Plaza de Cort. The tower stood at the farthest corner of the square from the Town Hall, on the site now occupied by a drug-merchant's shop. Calle Conquistador was until recently called 'The Street of St. Dominic's Poplars'.

Balearic Clock back only to the year 1385. They say that the Dominican Fathers bought and set it in the tower.[1]

This monastery of the Inquisition which is now a mere heap of wreckage, with here and there a scrubby tree or two and a few aromatic plants sprouting through the rubble, did not fall by the hand of time. Only a few years ago a readier and more merciless hand, the hand of revolution, pulled down and almost pulverized what is said to have been an architectural masterpiece. Certain fragments of rich mosaic and the skeletons of a few airy arches, still springing into the void, bear witness to its vanished splendour. The destruction throughout Spain of these repositories of Catholic art still excites indignant comment among the Palma aristocracy, and justifiable sorrow among artists. Were I ten years younger, I too might have been more struck by the vandalism of this destruction than by the page of history which it illustrates. Yet though there is good cause to lament—as M. Marliani does in his *Political History of Modern Spain*—the weak and at the same time violent side of the measures which this decree was destined to entail, I must confess that standing among these ruins I felt an emotion other than the sorrow usually aroused by ruins. Lightning had struck here, and lightning is a blind instrument, a force as savage as human anger; but the Providence that rules the elements and directs their apparent riotousness, is well aware that the beginnings of a new life are hidden under the ashes of ruin. On the day the monasteries fell, there was discernible in the political atmosphere of Spain something analogous to the need for renewal which Nature feels in her fruitful convulsions.

I refuse to believe what they told me in Palma: that this deed of violence was carried out before the eyes of the horrified people by a few malcontents greedy for revenge or booty. A great horde of malcontents are needed to break so huge an edifice into fragments, and only a people with very little feeling would stand and watch impassively the implementation of a decree that genuinely affronted them.

[1] Nobody seems to know what happened to the Clock; but I am assured that it is no longer in existence.

I am far readier to believe that the first stone torn from the top of these domes dislodged from the public heart a feeling of fear and awe no more firmly established there than was the monastic bell-tower on its foundations; and that each felt his innermost being stirred by a strange, sudden urge and sprang at the corpse with a mixture of courage and terror, rage and remorse. The monastic system sheltered many malpractices, and flattered much selfishness; religion is very powerful in Spain, and no doubt more than one destroyer repented next day and made his confession to the monk whom he had just hounded out of his sanctuary. But the most ignorant and blindest man has something in his heart which will make him tremble with enthusiasm when destiny confers a sovereign mission upon him.

With their pence and sweat the Spanish people had built these haughty palaces of the regular clergy, to whose gates they came century after century, craving the farthing of idle beggardom and the crust of intellectual servitude. They had been partners in the clergy's crime and shown equal cowardice. They had helped to pile up the faggots of the Inquisition. They had been abettors and informers in shocking persecutions of whole races which it was desired to extirpate. And after achieving the ruin of the Jews who had enriched them, and expelling the Moors[1] who had civilized them and made them great, they were chastised by Heaven with destitution and ignorance. Though single-minded and pious enough not to blame these clergy—their creatures, their corrupters and their scourge—but to endure for a long time, bowed beneath the yoke made by their own hands, nevertheless they one day heard strange, daring voices addressing their ears and hearts with words of liberation. They realized the mistake of their forebears, blushed at their own degradation, grew indignant at their own poverty, and despite their continued idolatrous attitude towards statues and relics, smashed these with a more abundant faith in human rights than in any religious creed.

What, then, is this secret power by which the prostrate votary

[1] The reference is to the Moriscoes, or converted Moors, expelled by Philip III of Spain in the early sixteenth century; Cervantes describes their expulsion, of which he heartily disapproved, in *Don Quixote*.

can all of a sudden be possessed, if only for a single day, and compelled to make a fanatic onslaught on the objects of his life-long worship?[1] It is certainly neither dissatisfaction with other people, nor weariness of inanimate things. It is dissatisfaction with oneself, weariness of one's own pusillanimity. And the Spanish people were greater on that day than is generally known. They performed a decisive deed and deprived themselves of the means of reneging, like a child who, wanting to be a man, breaks his toys and thus removes all temptation of turning to them again.

As for Don Juan Mendizábal—whose name is well worth mentioning in this context—he was a man of principles rather than of action, if my information about his political life is reliable. In my opinion, he over-rated the intellectual capacity of Spain at one period, and under-rated it at another; and that on occasion he took untimely or inadequate measures, sowing his ideas on barren fields where the seed must be choked or devoured, is perhaps sufficient reason to deny him the practical ability and inflexible nature needed for the immediate success of such undertakings. Yet this is no reason why history, regarded from a more philosophical point of view than is usual, should not one day hail him as one of the most generous and most enthusiastically progressive minds of Spain. At all events, M. Marliani's honesty of mind and lofty feeling for history prompted him to utter the following personal panegyric, while criticizing M. Mendizábal's government:

> . . . It will never be possible to deny M. Mendizábal these qualities, all the nobler for having been seldom encountered among his predecessors in office: a living faith in the future of the country, a boundless devotion to the cause of freedom, an ardent patriotism, and a genuine enthusiasm for progressive and even revolutionary ideas that might bring about the reforms for which the condition of Spain cried out aloud. He showed, moreover, tolerance, great generosity towards his foes; and finally an absence of personal ambition,

[1] This does not, however, seem to have been the case in Majorca. See footnote on p. 75.

which has at all times and in all circumstances made him sacrifice his individual interests to those of Spain, and so consistently as to leave him, at the close of his many ministries, without a single ribbon in his lapel. He was the first minister to take the regeneration of his country seriously. Mendizábal's term in office marked real progress. This time a minister spoke with the voice of the patriot. He was not strong enough to annul the Censorship, but he generously freed the Press from shackles, thus giving his enemies an advantage over himself. He submitted his administrative actions to the free scrutiny of public opinion; and when a violent opposition, instigated by his former friends, formed against him in Parliament, he magnanimously respected the rights of a certain deputy while the latter was acting in his official capacity. He told the House that he would rather cut off his right hand than sign an order for the dismissal of this deputy, whom he had once loaded with honours, but who had since become his bitterest political opponent. M. Mendizábal's noble example of tolerance deserves the greater praise in that such conduct was wholly unprecedented, and has since found no imitators.

I often pondered on this subject among the ruins of the Majorcan monasteries but although, when we heard Mendizábal's name cursed, it would have been awkward for us to defend it with praise and sympathy,[1] I told myself that, disregarding political issues of the day (for which I may be permitted to profess dislike and a studied ignorance) I could at least form a synthetic judgement on men and even on events, without fear of becoming ridiculous. It is not nearly so necessary, as some insist, to have first-hand knowledge of a nation, and to make an exhaustive study of its customs and material conditions, before attempting to form conceptions of its history and its future—in a word, of its spiritual life. It seems to me that there is one main line to follow in the general history of

[1] Mendizábal was a good friend both to Chopin, whom he had just accompanied to the Spanish frontier, and to George Sand. It appears that they carried letters of recommendation from him, and that these became a cause of embarrassment. He was now Spanish Ambassador at Paris.

human life, which is the same in every nation, and to which the threads of every private history are attached. This line is the awareness of and perpetual striving towards the ideal or (if you prefer the term) perfectibility, which men always carry within them, whether in the form of blind instinct or of brilliant theory. Every truly eminent person has felt this awareness and made some attempt at achievement; and those tc whom the vision has been most clearly revealed, and who have struck the boldest blows to hasten an ideal, are nearly always the ones most misjudged by their contemporaries. They have been slandered, misunderstood and condemned, and only when their labour has borne fruit have they been replaced on the pedestal from which a few transitory disappointments and a few unexplained setbacks had toppled them.

How many of our celebrated Revolutionary leaders have been belatedly and diffidently restored to deserved fame! And how little understood or developed their missionary work still remains! Mendizábal was one of Spain's most harshly-judged ministers, because he was the most courageous of them all, perhaps the only courageous one; and the deed that makes his short term in office unforgettable, the complete destruction of the monasteries, has been so severely censured that I feel compelled here to adduce in his defence the determination and delirious enthusiasm with which the Spanish people agreed to carry it out.

This, at any rate, is how I felt when I viewed these ruins, not yet blackened by Time and as it were themselves protesting against the past and heralding the dawn of truth in the hearts of the people. I refuse to believe that I have lost my taste and reverence for the arts; and I am not aware of harbouring revengeful and uncivilized instincts, like those who decry the worship of beauty and hold that we must turn our historic buildings into factories. In my view, however, an Inquisition monastery torn down by the people's hand is a no less magnificent, instructive and stirring page of history than a Roman aqueduct or amphitheatre. A cold-blooded governmental order, based on paltry utility or absurd economy, for the destruction of such a Temple would, of course, be an unpardonable outrage; but a political leader who, on a day of crisis, sacrifices art and science to the more valuable considerations of reason, justice and religious freedom; and a people who despite their religious instincts, their love of Catholic ceremonial and their reverence for monks, find sufficient strength of heart and hand to implement such a decree at a moment's notice, resemble the captain and his storm-tossed crew who save their lives by jettisoning their valuables.[1]

Weep then who will, over the ruins! Most of the buildings whose fall we lament were dungeons in which men's spirits or bodies had languished for centuries. And may there come poets who, rather than lament the passing of this world's infamy, will extol in their verse, over the broken fragments of gilded baubles and blood-stained rods, its manly coming of age. Adalbert Chamisso has written some fine verses on the subject of his ancestral château, destroyed in the French Revolution. His poem ends with a thought as novel in poetry as in politics:

> A blessing on you, ancient manor, over whom now the plough-share drives! And a blessing on him who drives the plough-share over you!

Having evoked the memory of this beautiful poem, should I dare copy out a few pages of prose inspired by my visit to a Dominican monastery? Why not? And why should the reader not show indulgence, when asked to pass judgement on something which the authoress has sacrificed her self-esteem and rooted inclinations to compose? I hope that the following fragment, for what it is worth, may introduce a little variety into the foregoing dry catalogue of buildings!

[1] The facts are these. No monastery of the Inquisition as such existed; but at Palma one or two Dominican fathers were Inquisitors. The Inquisition, an Ecclesiastical Court, handed over those it condemned to be dealt with by the secular arm of the Law: thus the prisons were not monastic prisons. It happened, however, that when the Liberals fell from office in 1823, several of their leaders were confined in the cells of the Dominican Monastery, and swore that if they ever returned to power they would raze the buildings. This they could do twelve years later; by implementing Mendizábal's decree. The work of destruction was allotted to a contractor. It remains a mystery who gave the order, which was unofficial; but the Madrid Government, when begged to preserve the monastery on artistic grounds, consented too late.

Chapter Eleven

The Monastery of the Inquisition

In the ruins of a monastery, two strangers met by the calm light of the moon. One appeared to be in the prime of life; the other, though bent beneath the weight of years, happened to be the younger of the two. Their encounter made them both tremble, for the hour was dark, the road lonely, and the Cathedral clock tolled the hour with slow and mournful strokes.

The bent stranger spoke first. 'Whoever you may be, sir,' he said, 'you have nothing to fear from a man so weak and crushed as myself. You can take nothing from me, either. I am poor and destitute.'

'Friend,' replied the other, 'my only enemies are those who attack me and, like you, I am too poor to fear robbers.'

'Then, brother, why did you start so at my approach?'

'Because, like all artists, I am somewhat superstitious, and mistook you for the ghost of one of those departed monks on whose shattered graves we are now treading. And you, friend, why did my approach equally startle you?'

'Because, being very superstitious, like all monks, I took you for the ghost of one of my fellows, who once buried me alive in the grave beneath your feet.'

'What? Are you then one of those men for whom I have eagerly and fruitlessly searched the land of Spain? Are you really a monk?'

'You will no longer find us anywhere under the light of the sun; but in the shadows of night you may still encounter us. Now your wish is granted; but what do you want with a monk?'

'I want to look at you and ask you questions, Father. I want to engrave your features on my memory and reproduce them in my painting. I want to gather up your words and repeat them to my fellow-countrymen. In short, I want to become acquainted with you, and be imbued with the mystery, poetry and greatness resident in the person of the monk and in the monastic life.'

'Where did you get such strange ideas, traveller? Do you not come from a land where Papal rule has been overthrown, the monks outlawed, and the monasteries suppressed?'

'There are still some among us who cherish a genuine feeling for the past, and whose eager imaginations are struck by the poetry of the Middle Ages. We seek out, respect, and almost adore everything that can waft us their fragrance, however faintly. Ah, Father, do not believe that we are all blind desecrators! We artists loathe the savages who pollute and break everything they touch. Far from approving their murderous decrees, we endeavour in our paintings, our poems, our dramas, and our other works to revivify the ancient traditions and the spirit of mysticism which will yet generate that sublime child, by name Christian Art!'

'What is all this, my son? Can it be that the artists of your free and prosperous country are going elsewhere for inspiration than to the present? With such an abundance of new things to sing, to paint, or celebrate, how can they be poring, as you say, over their ancestors' graves? How can they look for fruitful inspiration in that funereal dust, when God, in His goodness, has made their own age so sweet and gracious?'

'Your ideas of our age are somewhat unrealistic, good monk. We artists do not concern ourselves with politics; social questions interest us even less. We should be ill-advised to look for poetry in what goes on around us. The arts are sick, inspiration is smothered, bad taste triumphs, and the routine of everyday living absorbs all our faculties. Without the worship of the past and the monuments of centuried faith to invigorate us, the sacred fire which we struggle to keep alight would be extinguished for ever.'

'And yet they tell me that human genius has never made such

progress as with you in sociological science, in the marvels of industry and in the blessings of freedom. Have I been misinformed?'

'If you were told, Father, that at no previous time had such luxury and comfort ever been derived from material riches, or such an alarming variety of tastes, opinions and beliefs sprung from the collapse of pre-Revolutionary society, that was the truth. But if you were not told that all this, instead of making us happy, has merely debased and degraded us, you were not told the whole truth.'

'But what a strange result! How have the springs of happiness come to poison your lips? How have well-being and freedom made you mean and wretched rather than great, just and good? How do you account for this paradox?'

'Father, need I remind you that man does not live by bread alone? Since we have lost our faith, none of our discoveries has benefited our souls.'

'But have you lost your faith, my son, when religious persecutions are at an end, when you can expand your souls and raise your eyes towards the divine light? The moment of knowledge should have been the moment of belief. And yet you doubted? What clouded your spirits?'

'The cloud of human weakness and wretchedness. Investigation is surely not compatible with faith, Father?'

'Young man, you might as well ask me whether faith is compatible with truth! Do you then believe in nothing, my son? Or do you believe in falsehood?'

'Alas, I believe only in Art! But is that not sufficient to enrich the soul with strength, confidence and sublime joy?'

'Not so far as I know, my son. But I do not yet altogether understand. Are some of you still happy? Have you, for instance, contrived to avoid dejection and sorrow?'

'No, Father; artists are the most wretched, angry and tortured men of all, because each day they see the thing they worship sink a little lower, and are powerless to raise it up again whatever efforts they may exert.'

'But how is it that with such deep conviction as yours you artists can allow the arts to die out?'

'Because we lack faith, and without faith art cannot flourish.'

'Yet you have just told me that Art is your religion. Either this is a contradiction, my son, or else I am being stupid.'

'Of course we contradict ourselves, Father! We, to whom God has given a mission which the world refuses to let us pursue; we, for whom the present closes the door of fame, inspiration, and life; we, who are obliged to live in the past, and to seek from the dead the secrets of that eternal beauty whose altars the living have overturned and which they have forgotten how to worship. Standing before the great masterpieces of the past, and cherishing the pleasant hope of doing as well ourselves, we are filled with strength and enthusiasm; but when it comes to realizing our ambitious dreams, the cold winds of scorn and mockery blow on us from a sceptical and narrow-minded world. We cannot then produce work worthy of our ideal, and the concept dies darkly in our bosom before it can blossom in the light of day.'

The moon illumined the young artist's proud, melancholy face, and the motionless monk looked up at him with sweet simplicity, surprised at his bitterness.

'Let us sit here,' said the monk after a moment's silence, pausing beside the solid balustrade of a terrace that commanded the town, the countryside and the sea. This corner of the Dominicans' garden had lately been filled with flowers, fountains and valuable marbles, but was now strewn with debris and overrun by the tall weeds which grow with such vigour and speed among ruins.

In his excitement, the artist crushed one of these in his hand, and uttered a cry of pain as he flung it away. The monk smiled. 'That prick is sharp,' he said, 'but not dangerous. My son, the bramble which wounds you when you grasp it carelessly is symbolic of the coarse men who were just now the subject of your complaint. They overrun palaces and monasteries. They swarm upon the altars, and establish themselves on the wreckage of ancient glories. Look how these rank weeds have invaded the flower-beds, where not one of the valuable plants that we grew with such care has survived. Thus the simple, half-savage men who were driven from this garden like useless weeds have reasserted themselves, to choke one poisonous plant which grew in the shade and was called the Inquisition.'

'Why could they not have choked it without at the same time razing the sanctuaries of Christian art and the works of genius?'

'That accursed plant had to be torn up because it was both hardy and ubiquitous. The very foundations of these cloisters, under which its tap root lay hidden, had to be destroyed.'

'But, Father, of what beauty or use are these thorny weeds that have taken its place?'

The monk reflected for a moment before replying: 'Since you are a painter, you will doubtless sketch these ruins?'

'Certainly I shall. Why ask me that?'

'Will you, then, omit from your drawing those great brambles, hanging in festoons over the rubble, and swinging in the wind? Or will you welcome them as a felicitous detail in your composition, as Salvator Rosa did in a painting which I once saw?'

'They are an inseparable adjunct of the ruins. No painter could fail to make use of them.'

'In that case, they too have their beauty, their meaning and, logically, their use?'

'This argument does not improve your parable, Father. Sit beggars and gipsies among these ruins, and you will merely make the scene more sinister and desolate. A better picture will perhaps result; but how can it benefit mankind?'

'Yes, a better picture, perhaps; and certainly a most instructive one. Yet you artists, who provide the instruction, do not know what you are doing, and see nothing here but loose stones and growing grass.'

'Father, you are hard on me. Talk like yours provokes the reply that you saw nothing in this disaster except the destruction of your prison and the recovery of your freedom; for I suspect that the monastery was by no means to your liking.'

'And would you, my son, have carried your love of art and poetry so far as to live here contentedly?'

'I conceive of it as the most beautiful life in the world. Oh, what a noble monastery this must have been! How lofty its style! What splendours these ruins proclaim! How pleasant it must have been to come here of an evening, to enjoy a gentle breeze and the dreamy sound of the sea. When these airy galleries were paved with rich mosaics, when crystalline waters babbled in marble pools, and a silver lamp shone like a pale star in the heart of the sanctuary! What peace, what august silence, you must have enjoyed when the reverence and trust of your people surrounded you with an impregnable wall, when they lowered their voices and crossed themselves each time they passed before your mysterious portals! Oh, who would not gladly renounce all the cares, strains and ambitions of social life if he might come and bury himself here, in tranquil oblivion of the whole world, and be an artist: able to devote ten, perhaps even twenty, years to a single painting, which he would polish slowly like a precious stone, and which he would at last see set upon an altar, not to be judged and criticized by every ignoramus, but to be hailed and invoked as an image worthy of the Deity itself.'

'Stranger,' the monk replied severely, 'your words are arrogant and your dreams vain indeed! In this art of which you speak so grandiloquently, and which you exalt so high, you see only your own hand, and the solitude for which you hanker would be no more to you than a means of exalting and deifying yourself. I now understand how you can believe in this selfish Art, without any religious faith or social sense. But have you considered the matter closely? Are you aware of what took place in these dens of corruption and terror? Come with me, and perhaps what I am going to show you will make you think differently.'

The monk led our young traveller, not without danger, across precipitous mounds of loose rubble, to the centre of the ruined monastery, where the prisons had been, and guided him carefully along the side of a solid mass of masonry fourteen feet thick, which pick and shovel had split open. In the heart of this terrifying crust of stone and cement gaped dark, airless cells, separated from one another by blocks as thick as the keystones of their dismal vaults.

'Young man,' said the monk, 'these pits are not wells, nor even graves; they are the dungeons of the Inquisition. Here all who dared think differently from the Holy Office died a gradual death, whether they were guilty or innocent in the eyes of God, whether they were debased by vice, distraught by passion, or inspired by genius and virtue.

'These Dominican fathers were scholars, men of letters, even artists. In their enormous libraries, theological subtleties bound in gilt morocco reposed on ebony shelves, their margins glittering with pearls and rubies. Yet they relegated Man, that living book in which God Himself recorded His thoughts, to an obscure existence in the bowels of the earth. They owned vessels of chased silver, chalices sparkling with precious stones, splendid pictures, gold and ivory Madonnas, and yet Man, that chosen vessel, that chalice brimming with heavenly grace, that living image of God, they consigned alive to the chill of death and the worms of the tomb! Some of them tended roses and jonquils with as much loving care as a mother bestows on her child, yet felt no pity when they beheld their fellow-man, their brother, grown pale and rotting in the dank tomb.

'That, my son, was the way of monks and monasteries! Brutal savagery alternating with spineless cowardice; selfish intelligence combined with ruthless piety, that was the Inquisition. And since, while opening these foul pits to the light of Heaven, the hand of deliverance shook down a few pillars, or dulled a few patches of gilt, must we clap back the tombstone over the dying victims? Must we bewail the fate of their torturers, deprived of gold and slaves?'

The artist had descended into one of the vaults to examine its walls. For a moment he tried to envisage the struggle which the human will, buried alive, could maintain against the terrible despair of such a captivity. But no sooner had his impressionable imagination painted this picture, than it was filled with distress and terror. He felt those icy vaults weighing down his soul, he trembled in every limb, he could not breathe, his strength ebbed away as he tried to leap out of the abyss and, stretching his arms towards the monk, who had remained on the brink, he cried out: 'In the name of Heaven, Father, help me to escape from here!'

'My son,' said the monk, extending his hand, 'if you are relieved at the sight of the stars shining overhead, imagine my relief when I saw the sun again, after ten years of torment!'

'Unhappy monk!' exclaimed the artist, hurrying back to the garden. 'Could you, indeed, endure ten years of death in life and keep your sanity? Had I stayed there a moment longer, be sure I should have become an idiot or a madman. Never could I have thought that the sight of a dungeon would arouse such sudden stark terror in me! I do not understand how the mind can grow accustomed and resigned to such a fate. At Venice, I saw the instruments of torture, the dungeons of the Ducal Palace, and the dark blind alley where victims fell, struck by an unseen hand. I was shown the perforated flagstone, through which their blood dripped into the canal and left no trace; it gave me the impression of a more or less speedy death. But that dungeon of yours, it is the idea of life that terrifies the mind. Oh, God! To be there and unable to die!'

'Look at me, my son,' said the monk, uncovering his bald, wrinkled head. 'I have lived no longer than you—you with the virile face and untroubled brow—yet, doubtless, I am an old man in your eyes. It matters little what I did to deserve my slow torment, or how I endured it. I do not ask for pity; I no longer need it, so gay and young does the sight of these toppled walls and empty dungeons make me feel. Nor do I wish to inspire in you a horror of the monks; they are free, and so am I, for God is good to all. But, being an artist, you will have profited by experiencing an emotion necessary to the performance of the tasks that you set yourself.

'If you now paint these ruins where you wished to weep for the past, and where I come every night to throw myself down and thank God for the present, your genius will be inspired, perhaps, by loftier feelings than faint-hearted regret or sterile rapture. Some buildings, though of inestimable value to antiquaries, have no other merit than that of recalling the deeds which humanity consecrated by their erection, and these were often wicked or childish. Since you have travelled, you may have seen at Genoa a bridge with enormous piers, which a vain aristocrat threw over a chasm, and on the other side the sumptuous, graceless and costly church he built, in an uninhabited district, because he was too vain either to kneel in a church beside the members of his parish, or ford the stream for worship elsewhere. Perhaps you have also seen the Egyptian pyramids, those terrifying witnesses to the slavery of nations; or the dolmens, once drenched in human blood so that the unquenchable thirst of cruel gods might be slaked. But most of you artists have eyes only for beautiful or curiously executed crafts, and are impervious to the ideas that this work substantiates. Hence your intellect often worships the visible manifestation of emotion which your heart, if aware of it, would reject.

'Thus your own works are frequently untrue to the colour of life, especially when, disregarding the blood that courses in the veins of live men, you interpret the dead with cold and deliberate miscomprehension.'

'Father,' answered the young man, 'I do not entirely reject your lesson; but how can Art draw inspiration from such a philosophy? You are using today's reason to expound a doctrine conceived in poetic frenzy by the resourceful superstition of our fathers. If we were to replace the smiling deities of Greece with the commonplace allegories concealed beneath their voluptuous lines; if, instead of the divine Madonna of the Florentine School, we were to paint a sturdy ale-wench in the Dutch style; finally, if we turned Jesus, the Son of God, into a naïve Platonic philosopher, we should lose our godhead and be left only with man; just as here, instead of a Christian church, we gaze upon a heap of shattered stones.'

'My son,' replied the monk, 'the Florentines gave the Virgin divine features because they still believed in her; and if the Dutch gave her common features, that was because they no longer believed in her. And if you and your contemporaries, though believing only in art, that is to say, in individual creation, flatter yourselves that you are going to paint sacred subjects, success will elude you. So do not flee into the past from what is palpably alive and of the present day.

'Had I been an artist, I should have devoted a splendid picture to the theme of liberation: painting bold, sturdy men with hammers grasped in their right hands and torches in their left, as they broke into this limbo which I have just shown you, and resurrected from the befouled flagstones ghosts with dulled eyes and scared smiles. I should have shown the light of Heaven falling on my rescuers through the cracked vaults, a halo about their heads. A subject truly well-suited to my times, as Michelangelo's Last Judgement was to his; for my unlettered deliverers, whom you despise as coarse and brutal vandals, seemed nobler and fairer to me than all the angels of Heaven. Indeed, I find this ruin, which you view with melancholy dismay, a more sacred monument than it ever was before its fall.

'Were it my task to raise an altar that should bear witness to future generations of the greatness and power of our own, I should ask for nothing better than this mound of wreckage, above which I should set a consecrated stone with this inscription: "Here, in the days of ignorance and cruelty, men worshipped a God of revenge and torture. On the Day of Justice, and in the name of Humanity, men overturned these bloodstained altars, hateful to the God of Mercy!" '

Chapter Twelve

It was not in Palma, but in the ruined House of the Inquisition at Barcelona, that I saw those dungeons which had been enclosed in solid blocks of masonry fourteen feet thick. It may well be that when the people of Palma broke open the similar dungeons in the monastery of St. Dominic they were found to be empty; and I must apologize, as is only proper, to the susceptible Majorcans for the poetic licence I have taken in the previous chapter.

However, every invention has a certain foundation of truth, and I may mention that I met a priest in Majorca, now the rector of a Palma parish, who told me that he had spent seven years of his life, the flower of his youth, in prisons of the Holy Office, and was released only through the influence of a lady who had held him in affectionate respect. He was then still fairly young, with animated eyes and vivacious bearing and did not appear greatly to regret the passing of the so-called Holy Office. As for this Dominican monastery, let me quote a passage from M. Grasset, which is plainly unbiased, since introduced by a high-flown panegyric of the Majorcan Inquisitors whom he had met:

> . . . However, in the cloisters of St. Dominic reminders of the former atrocities committed against the Jews are still to be seen. Each of the unfortunate victims figures in a picture, at the foot of which are written his name, age, and the date when he was burned. I was assured that a few years ago the descendants of these hapless men, who now form a separate class among the inhabitants of Palma,

under the absurd name of 'screech-owls',[1] had offered considerable sums to have these distressing records obliterated, but without success. . . . This I declined to believe. . . . Yet I shall never forget how one day, as I strolled in the Dominican cloisters, sorrowfully examining those sad pictures, a monk came up to me and pointed out that several of them were marked with cross-bones. 'These,' he said, 'are the heretics whose ashes were exhumed and cast to the winds.' My blood ran cold; I left abruptly, cut to the heart and stricken to the soul.

I chanced to come across a report printed in 1755, by order of the Inquisition. It contained the names, surnames, occupations and offences of all the unfortunates on whom sentence was passed in Majorca between the years 1645 and 1691. I shuddered as I read this document. I found that four Majorcans, one a woman, had been burned alive for Judaism, thirty-two others had died for the same offence, in the Inquisition dungeons, and their bodies had been burned; in three cases the ashes were exhumed and cast to

[1] In 1453, the great mass of Jews at Palma, whose ancestors had first emigrated there as early as the reign of Claudius, were forced by penal laws to apostatize. The Goldsmiths' Guild contrived to keep their faith until, under Philip II, they were given the alternatives of conversion, emigration or burning at the stake. Some emigrated; some made a real or pretended adhesion to Catholicism. According to a popular etymology of the name *xueta* (which has been misunderstood as equivalent to the French word *chouetta*, screech-owl), converts found it politic to sit in front of their workshops and ostentatiously eat *chuletas* (pork chops) to prove that they had forsaken the Law. But *xueta* is merely a corruption of *jueto* (Jew). In the late seventeenth century a group of *xuetas* was found to be still secretly practising Judaism; the punishments inflicted on them are the subject of M. Grasset's account. Messrs Tous of Palma have recently published the original documents in two small volumes. The *Xuetas*, who are concentrated in two streets, and remain goldsmiths, are a closely-knit community. One of them sold me a silver sixteenth-century Lion of Judah, the ornament of a Torah Scroll, without knowing in the least what it represented. Until recently they married only among themselves and were despised by the rest of Palma; the popular superstition being that because their ancestors spat at Jesus during the Crucifixion they cannot now control their spittle. There is strong historical evidence for supposing that Cristobal Colom (Christopher Columbus) was a Majorcan Jew; his surname is still common in the island. Part of a pre-Conquest Jewish synagogue has been incorporated in the fabric of Montesion Church.

the winds. Moreover, a Dutchman charged with Lutheranism; a Majorcan charged with Mohammedanism; six Portuguese, including a woman, and seven Majorcans, charged with Judaism; were all burned in effigy, having had the good fortune to escape. I counted two hundred and sixteen other victims, Majorcans and foreigners, charged with Judaism, heresy or Mohammedanism, who were released from prison after having publicly recanted and returned to the bosom of the Church.

This ghastly catalogue wound up with a no less shocking decree of the Inquisition:

'All the offenders listed in this report have been publicly sentenced by the Holy Office, as avowed heretics; their possessions confiscated and devoted to the Royal Treasury; themselves pronounced incompetent and disqualified from holding or acceding to any rank or benefices, whether ecclesiastical or secular, or any other public offices or honours; unfit to carry on their persons, or have carried by their dependants, gold, silver, pearls, precious stones, coral, silk, camlet, or broadcloth; to ride on horseback, carry arms, or practise and use the other things which, by common law, the laws and pragmatic sanctions of this Kingdom, or the directions and style of the Holy Office, are prohibited to persons thus degraded; the same prohibition extending, in the case of women under sentence of burning, to their sons and their daughters, and in the case of men, down to the third generation in tail male; condemning at the same time the memory of those executed in effigy, ordaining that their bones (provided that these can be distinguished from those of faithful Christians) shall be exhumed, handed over to justice and to the secular arm, to be burned and reduced to ashes; and there shall be obliterated or scraped away all inscriptions appearing in the burial-places of the said heretics, wherever they may be, whether affixed, or painted, and all armorial bearings, so that there remain nothing of them on the face of the earth, except the memory of their sentence and of their execution.'

When one reads documents as recent as these,[1] and observes the relentless hatred by which the unhappy Jews are still pursued in Majorca, even after twelve to fifteen generations of conversion to Christianity, it is hard to believe that the spirit of the Inquisition had died out there so entirely as was said at the time of Mendizábal's decree.[2]

I shall finish this subject by acquainting the reader with a rather curious discovery, the whole credit for which belongs to M. Tastu, and which would have made that scholar's fortune thirty years ago, unless he had taken it, lightheartedly and without a thought of recompense, to the then Master of the World —which is probably what he would have done because, like all true artists, he had a carefree and easy-going nature. This note is too interesting to be curtailed by me. Here it is, exactly as it was placed into my hands, with permission to publish it.

Monastery of St. Dominic at Palma, Majorca

Miguel de Fabra, a comrade of St. Dominic, founded the Majorcan Order of preaching friars. He came from Old Castile and, in 1229, accompanied James I in the conquest of the Great Balearic. His knowledge was deep and varied, and his piety remarkable; which gave him a strong hold over the Conqueror, the nobles who accompanied him, and even the common soldiery. He would not only preach to the troops, hold divine services, and dispense Holy Communion, but fight against the infidels as was then the custom of the clergy. The Moors maintained that the Blessed Virgin and Father Miguel alone had conquered them. Aragonese and Catalan soldiers would address their prayers, it is said, after God and the Blessed Virgin, to Father Miguel Fabra. This famous Dominican had received the

[1] George Sand's patriotism and progressive ardour make her forget the horrors of the Terror which had taken place in Paris less than fifty years before she visited Majorca.

[2] Most Majorcans say: 'To every man his own religion.' It is only from ritual conservatism that every Holy Thursday an immense procession of *Cofradias*, religious brotherhoods of Palma, winds penitentially through the city, dressed in long, shapeless habits and eye-holed hoods of the Inquisitors. Among them is a *Cofradia* of *Xuetas*; they are now notoriously the most pious Catholics in Palma.

habit of his order at Toulouse from the hands of his friend Dominic; and been sent by him to Paris with two others on an important mission. It was he who established the first Dominican monastery at Palma, which was endowed by the Bursar of the first Bishop of Majorca, Don J. R. de Torella, and placed under the charge of his brother; this was in the year 1231.

A mosque and a few perches of land belonging to it were used for the first foundation. Later, the preaching friars enlarged their community, by a profitable trade in every kind of commodity, and by the fairly frequent donations of the faithful. Miguel de Fabra's brother, however, had gone to die in Valencia, which he had helped to conquer. The architect was Jaime Fabra. He is not said to have been related to Father Miguel, his namesake; but is known to have handed in his plans about the year 1296, and later drafted those of Barcelona Cathedral and of several other Cathedrals in the Aragonese dominions. The monastery and its church must have suffered many vicissitudes in the course of time, as is apparent if you compare the different features of the ruined buildings, as we have done. Here are the tottering relics of a sumptuous main door whose style savours of the fourteenth century; but farther on, shattered arches and cumbrous keystones lying in the wreckage, proclaim themselves the work of other architects, considerably inferior to Jaime Fabra.

Over these vast ruins, where nothing has remained upright except a few centenarian palm-trees, preserved at our urgent plea, we were able to lament (as we did over the ruins of the Convent of Santa Catalina in Barcelona) that these undiscriminating acts of destruction were directed only by the cold hand of the politician. As a matter of fact, art and history have lost little by the fall of the Monasteries of San Jeronimo at Palma, or that of San Francisco, which obstructed the neighbouring sea-wall at Barcelona. But, in the name of history, in the name of art, why could they not have preserved as historic buildings, the Convent of Santa Catalina at Barcelona and the Dominican Monastery at Palma, 'whose aisles sheltered the tombs of noble folk,' as is said in a note-book taken from the monastery archives, which we have examined? These tombs are listed and, after the name of N. Cotoner, Grand-Master of

Malta, occur those of persons belonging to the Dameto, Muntaner, Villalonga, La Romana, and Bonapart families! The notebook, together with everything else contained in the monastery, now belongs to the contractor who undertook to demolish it.[1]

This typical Majorcan, whose manner at first startles you but afterwards sets you at ease by its charm, seeing the interest we took in these historic ruins and also being like all members of the lower classes, an admirer of the great Napoleon, eagerly showed us the tomb adorned with what Majorcan tradition affirms to be the heraldic bearings of his Bonapart ancestors. We found this remarkable enough to justify a certain amount of research on the subject; but the pressure of other work denied us the time and care needed for its completion.

Nevertheless, we have traced the armorial bearings of the Bonaparts. They are as follows: *Parti per pale azure and gules: on the first, six mullets or, displayed by two, two and two; on the second, a lion leopardy or; on a chief or, an eagle nascent sable.*[2] We took a facsimile of this coat from a Spanish armigery, or book of heraldry, which was one of the most valuable objects contained in the library of the Count of Montenegro. At Barcelona, in another, less beautifully-produced Spanish armigery, belonging to the learned keeper of Public Records for the Aragonese

[1] So the work of destruction, it is now admitted, was done by a contractor's gang, not by the hands of a nobly enthusiastic mob, as George Sand has hitherto contended. Spontaneous violence is foreign to the Majorcans; but they are so law-abiding that if they saw a gang of men dynamiting the Cathedral and claiming to be acting under orders, they would shrug, murmur 'What a pity!', and move out of range. Much the same seems to have happened in 1835.

[2] This means: Shield divided vertically, two-thirds of the way down, into two parts, one blue, one red. On the blue part, six stars are arranged in pairs. On the red is a lion, walking and with its head turned full face. The top third of the shield is gold-coloured and shows a black eagle in the act of rising. M. Tastu's reproduction of the shields do not, however, correspond with the blazoning. The Fortuny armigery shows five, not six, stars which are black, not gold; and the background is gold, not red; also the lion stands on a red, not a blue, background; in the Dameto armigery, the colours are correctly blazoned but the lion (as also in the Fortuny armigery) is rampant, not leopardy

J. B. Rietstap's *Armorial Générale* (V. and H. Rolland's edition) agrees with the blazoning of the Dameto armigery, except that the eagle is described as *displayed*, i.e. spread out as if nailed to a barn door, not nascent. That the mullets are six-pointed (not five-pointed) shows that this is a French coat.

Crown, we find, dated June 15th, 1549, the proofs of the Fortuny family's noble extraction, among which appears, as one of their four quarterings, that of the maternal grandmother, who was a Bonapart.

In the register named *Index: Pedro III*, which forms the second volume of the Aragonese Royal Records, two deeds dated 1276 are mentioned, relating to certain members of the Bonpar family. This name, originating in Provençal or Languedoc, would have become Bonapart when modified by the Majorcans, as were many others at that date. In 1411, Hugh Bonapart, a native of Majorca, migrated to the island of Corsica in the capacity of Regent or Governor for King Martin of Aragon, and the origin of the Corsican Bonapartes or, as they were later called, Buonapartes, is ascribable to him; thus, Bonapart is the Romance name, Bonaparte the old Italian, and Buonaparte the modern Italian. The members of Napoleon's family are known to have signed themselves indifferently Bonaparte or Buonaparte.

Who knows what importance these slight discoveries might have gained a few years earlier, had they served to prove that the family of Napoleon, who set such store by his French nationality,[1] originated in France. M. Tastu's find is no less interesting for not having the same political importance today, and if I had a voice in the disbursement of Government funds allocated to the Humanities, I should provide him with the means of completing his researches. There is little point now, I agree, in ascertaining the French origin of Napoleon. He was a great commander and, though not to my mind such a great prince—I humbly apologize for this unfashionable judgement—most certainly a great man, and well and truly adopted by France. Posterity will not ask whether his ancestors came from Florence, Corsica, Majorca or Languedoc; but historians will be interested in raising the veil that shrouds this predestined family, for which the birth of Napoleon was most certainly not a chance contingency, a disconnected event. I am convinced that a careful search among the earlier generations would reveal men or

[1] He could also claim British nationality, Corsica having been briefly part of the British Empire.

women worthy of such progeny, and in this case the coat of arms, hereditary insignia which the Law of Equality has treated as they deserve,[1] but which the historian must always regard as memorials of the greatest significance, might well cast some light on the wars and ambitions of earlier Bonapartes.[2]

Yet was there ever a prouder and more symbolic escutcheon than that of these Majorcan knights? The lion in the attitude of combat,[3] the sky studded with stars from which the prophetic eagle seeks to break away,[4] is surely, so to speak, the enigmatical hieroglyph of a more than ordinary destiny? It may be that Napoleon, who had an almost superstitious love for stars, and who gave France the eagle for her emblem, was aware of his Majorcan escutcheon and, having been unable to trace it to the presumed original Bonparo of Provence, kept quiet about his Spanish ancestors. It is the fate of great men, once they are dead, to watch the nations quarrelling over their cradles or their graves.

[1] They were banned at the French Revolution.

[2] George Sand had generously praised Napoleon III's writings while he was still a political prisoner. In 1851, when he became Dictator, she reminded him of the warm correspondence they had exchanged and persuaded him to revoke the sentences of death or exile against numbers of her Republican associates. A similar service was done her by Prince Jerome Bonaparte in Africa.

[3] If rampant; if leopardy, then merely active and watchful, like the three *lions leopardy* on the English Royal arms.

[4] George Sand was no herald. The stars belong to a different part of the shield; the eagle is nascent from a dawn sky.

Chapter Thirteen

It was a cloudless mid-December[1] morning during one of those beaming spells of autumn sunshine which soon became more and more uncommon, and we set out for Valldemosa to take possession of our Carthusian cell. After crossing the fertile plain of Establiments, we reached an indeterminate terrain, here covered with trees, there dry and stony, there again moist and fresh—everywhere shifting its character with an abruptness that I have never seen paralleled elsewhere. In no other country, unless perhaps in some of the Pyrenean valleys, had Nature shown herself to me with such free allure as on these heathlands, which spread over a fairly wide area and struck me as repudiating the Majorcans' boast that the whole of their island has been reduced to a perfect state of cultivation.[2]

However, I did not think of holding this against them, since nothing is more beautiful than neglected lands like these, which grow all that they desire, without need of more: twisted, bent, dishevelled trees; frightful thorns, splendid flowers; carpets of mosses and rushes, prickly caper-bushes, delicate asphodels; all creation appearing there in the forms God has given them—a gully, a hill, a stony path which slips without warning into a ravine, a green track plunging into a deceptive stream, a meadow open to all comers but suddenly arrested by the face of a precipitous mountain; then woods strewn with great rocks seemingly fallen from the sky, sunken roads running beside the torrent between bushes of myrtle and woodbine; and finally a

[1] December 18th, 1838. They stayed for fifty-six days.

[2] The approaches to the Valldemosa pass, being unsuitable for ploughland, are still used for pasture.

farmhouse dropped like an oasis in the heart of this wilderness, its palm-tree a watch-tower to guide the solitary traveller.

Neither Switzerland nor the Tyrol had shown this aspect of free, primeval creation which was so delightful in Majorca. It seemed to me that in the wildest parts of the Swiss mountains Nature, too roughly treated by atmospheric influences, had eluded the hand of man only to meet with more rigorous coercion from the sky, and to become enslaved by her self-lacerations, like a passionate spirit left to its own devices. In Majorca, she blooms beneath the kisses of a burning sky, and smiles beneath the gusts of warm winds that brush over her as they roam the seas. Flowers though beaten down spring up more sturdily than before; tree-trunks broken by the storm put forth more shoots than ever; and although there is, strictly speaking, no desert in Majorca, the lack of regular roads gives it an abandoned and rebellious look. The landscape must have something in common with those beautiful savannahs of Louisiana where, among vivid dreams of my youth, I used to follow with René when he tracked the footprints of Atala or Chactas.

I am pretty sure that this panegyric would give little pleasure to the Majorcans, who claim that their roads are very pleasant. Pleasant to look at, admittedly: but you shall judge for yourselves whether they are negotiable by wheeled transport.

The local hackney carriage is the *tartana*, a kind of springless post-chaise drawn by a horse or mule; or the *birlucho*,[1] a kind of gig, which seats four and rests on its shafts like the tartana. Both are provided with solid wheels and massive iron fittings, and their interiors are upholstered with six inches of flock stuffing. Such cushioning certainly gives you food for thought when you install yourself for the first time in this tempting conveyance. The driver sits on a plank which serves him as a box, his feet straddling the shafts, while the animal runs between his legs, so that he has the advantage of experiencing every movement it makes, as well as every bump of his barrow: thus he drives a coach and rides a horse at the same time. This odd means of travel does not, however, seem to incommode him, because he sings the whole time, though dreadfully jolted; and interrupts

[1] More correctly: *birlocxo*.

his song only to utter terrifying oaths,[1] if his beast hesitates on the brink of a precipice or at the foot of a rock-wall.

This is how one goes driving: ravines, torrents, swamps, quickset hedges, ditches, all bar the path in vain; one does not stop for such trifles because, of course, they are all part of the road. At the outset, you may believe that this steeplechase is a wager in bad taste, and ask your guide what fly has bitten him. 'We are on the road,' he answers. 'But that river?' 'It is part of the road.' 'And that deep hole?' 'Part of the road.' 'And that thicket?' 'All part of the road.' 'Fine!'

Then you are left with no alternative but to resign yourself to your fate, bless the upholstery without which your limbs could not fail to be broken, commit your soul to God, and contemplate the scenery either in expectation of death or in hope of a miracle. And yet you often reach your destination safe and sound, thanks to the steadiness of the carriage, the strength of the horse's legs, and perhaps also the indifference of the driver, who lets the beast pick its own way while he sits with folded arms phlegmatically smoking his cigar, though one wheel may run on a mountain and the other in a ravine.

A risk faced by others soon ceases to appear dangerous: and yet the danger is very real. You do not always overturn; but when that happens you are seldom righted.[2] M. Tastu had experienced such an accident, a year before, on our road to Establiments, and been left for dead where he lay. He afterwards suffered from terrible headaches which did not, however, damp his desire to visit the island again.

Almost everyone in Majorca owns a carriage of some sort, and the nobility fancy those Louis XIV coaches, with bell-mouthed boxes, as many as eight windows, and huge wheels which defy all obstacles. These heavy, lumbering contraptions, badly sprung, but roomy and strong, are nimbly drawn by four or six stout mules, and will convey you at a gallop with incredible daring through the most frightful gorges: not that you escape

[1] The stock oath for a mule is: 'Forty basketfuls of harlots!'

[2] According to the opening chapter of *Pickwick Papers*, which refers to the contemporary English scene, the overturning of postchaises was a daily hazard on country roads near London.

without a few bruises, bumps on your head, or at the very least an agonizing stiffness.

The sober and humourless Miguel de Vargas, a typical Spanish author, writes in the following terms of the 'horrible roads' of Majorca: 'It is impossible sufficiently to emphasize the neglect of this essential branch of organization. . . . What they call a road is a string of impassable precipices, and the unfortunate traveller journeying from Palma to the hills of Galatzo is confronted with death at every step. . . .'

Near Palma, the roads are a little less perilous, but have the serious disadvantage of being so narrowly confined between walls or ditches that two vehicles which meet cannot pass. The oxen must then be unhitched from the cart, or the horses from the carriage, and one of the two turn-outs must then be reversed, often for a long distance. Endless disputes arise as to which party shall give way; and during this delay the traveller is obliged to repeat for his own edification the Majorcan motto: *Mucha calma.*[1]

Though the Majorcans spend so little money on the upkeep of their roads, they have the advantage of possessing these in plenty. In fact, there is only too great a choice. I journeyed no more than three times from our monastery to Palma, and back again; but I took six different roads, and on every occasion the driver of the *birlucho* lost his way and took us wandering up hill and down dale in pretended search of a seventh road, said to be the best of all, which he never found.[2]

At this point you begin to realize that you are on the Alpine side of Majorca; but however steeply the mountains rise on either side of the gorge, however furiously the torrents may

[1] This happened to me the other day on the main Valldemosa-Deyá road, at a point between a stone wall and an unprotected terrace. The bus in which I travelled was going downhill and therefore had precedence; the other vehicle was driven by a young farmer, who was taking back a party of girl olive-pickers to their village and did not want to be laughed at for giving way. The presence in the bus of a priest, friendly to the farmer, and of a *guardia* who knew the law, did not help matters. After an argument lasting half an hour, the farmer backed his car five yards and we passed.

[2] The trunk roads of the island, including the Palma-Valldemosa stretch, now compare very favourably with those of the mainland; but many large villages on the plain are still connected only by narrow dirt-tracks.

leap from boulder to boulder, it is only in the depth of winter that these regions take on the wild appearance which the Majorcans ascribe to them. In the month of December, despite recent rains, the torrent was still no more than a delightful stream flowing through clumps of grasses and flowers; the mountain smiled, and the narrow vale of Valldemosa opened before us like a spring garden.

To reach the Charterhouse, one has to alight at the foot of the hill on which it stands; for no cart can climb the paved road which boldly winds in and out among beautiful trees, while enchanting scenery unfolds at each step, growing lovelier and lovelier the higher one climbs. I have seen nothing more inviting, yet at the same time more melancholy, than these steep slopes where the varied tints of holm-oak, carob-tree, pine, olive, poplar and cypress blend in thick arbours, unfathomable depths of greenery, and the torrent plunges headlong through groves of lavish exuberance and incomparable grace. I shall never forget a bend of the pass where a backward glance reveals one of those charming Arab cottages I have described, perched on a hill, half-hidden among its jointed prickly-pears, and dominated by a tall palm-tree which leans over the chasm, its silhouette black against the heavens. When depressed by the mire and fog of Paris, I close my eyes and see again, as in a dream, that green mountain, those tawny rocks, and the single palm-tree lost in a rosy sky.

The Valldemosa range rises in a series of narrow plateaux to a sort of corrie formed by high mountains and closed on the northern side by the slope of a final plateau, the approaches to the monastery. With vast labour, the Carthusians softened the harshness of this romantic place. They converted the higher part of the valley into an extensive garden by terrace-walls which leave the view unobstructed. A border of pyramidal cypresses, ranged in pairs on various levels, gives it the contrived look of a cemetery at the Opera.

This garden, planted with palms and almond-trees, begins at the bottom slope of the hill, and rises in huge, ever-steepening tiers which, by moonlight, when their asymmetricality is shrouded in shadow, suggest an amphitheatre hewn for contests between giants. In the middle, beneath a group of fine palm-trees, a stone tank collects the waters of the mountain streams and discharges them to the lower plateaux through conduits made of stone flags, like those that irrigate the Barcelona countryside. These conduits are too extensive and ingenious, in Majorca as in Catalonia, to be the work of any nation except the Moors. They cover the whole interior of the island; those which start from the Carthusians' garden and run beside the bed of the torrent, convey spring water to Palma throughout the year.[1]

Beyond the monastery, to the north, the pass becomes a broad valley; this widens as it slopes gently down on the other side of the hill towards the steep coastal cliffs, at whose feet the sea pounds and corrodes. One branch of the range goes off in the general direction of Spain; the other towards the east.[2] Hence this picturesque Charterhouse commands the sea on both sides. The waves thunder in one's ears from the north, and one can glimpse a faint glittering line beyond the entrance to the pass, and the vast plain unfolding to the south. It is a sublime picture: the foreground framed by dark, fir-covered rocks, the middle distance by bold mountains fringed with stately trees, the near background by rounded hillocks which the setting sun gilds warmly, and on whose crests the eye can make out, though a league away, the outlines of microscopic trees, delicate as a butterfly's antennae, but as sharply black as the stroke of a pen in Indian ink on a field of sparkling gold. Behind these stretches the plain; and at this distance, when the mountain mists begin to rise and cast a transparent veil over the depths, anyone would take it for the sea. Yet the sea lies still farther in the background and, when the sun returns in the morning and the plain resembles a blue lake, the Mediterranean sets a limit to this dazzling vista with a strip of brilliant silver.

It is one of those overwhelming views that leave nothing to be desired, nothing to the imagination. Whatever poet and painter might dream, Nature has here created: vast general effect, countless detail, inexhaustible variety, blurred shapes, bold

[1] This is wholly untrue. Valldemosa has never supplied Palma with water.

[2] No: one branch runs north-east, the other south-west; 'the general direction of Spain' is north-west.

outlines, hazy depths—everything! Art could never add anything to it. Our minds cannot always appreciate and understand the work of God, and when we reflect seriously upon ourselves, we realize the impossibility of ever expressing creatively this infinitude of life which enthrals and intoxicates us. I should advise those who are consumed by artistic vainglory to look well and often at such scenes; and thus acquire a certain respect for the divine art that directs the eternal creation of things—a respect in which, as I judge from their vainglorious behaviour, they are singularly lacking. For myself, I never felt the emptiness of words more keenly than in my hours of meditation at this monastery. Religious impulses came on me frequently; but the only form of words found to express my enthusiasm was: 'Blessed be Thou, God, Who hast given me good eyes!'

Yet I believe that while the occasional enjoyment of these sublime sights is invigorating and beneficial, danger lies in their permanent possession. One grows accustomed to living beneath the sway of one's senses, and all sensuous over-indulgence is punished by the law of nervous irritation. This explains why monks, on the whole, take little interest in the poetry of their monasteries, or peasants and herdsmen in the beauty of their mountains.[1] We ourselves escaped because almost every evening the mist would descend, hastening the fall of what little daylight our hollow allowed us. Until midday we were overshadowed by the high mountain to our left, and at three o'clock fell into the shadow of the other high mountain to our right. But what lovely plays of light we were able to study, when rays came slanting through the cleft rocks or gliding between the mountain ridges, to touch the middle-distance with crests of gold and purple! Sometimes the tops of our cypresses, dark obelisks acting as foils to the background, were bathed in this liquid glow; the clusters of dates[2] on our palm-trees seemed clusters of rubies, and a long line of shadow, cutting obliquely

[1] Coleridge had anticipated George Sand, holding that love of mountain scenery was a purely literary emotion: '. . . Among the peasantry of North Wales the ancient mountains with all their terrors and all their glories are pictures to the blind and music to the deaf.'

[2] Dates never ripen properly in Majorca, but are harvested and sold to children from barrows. Their best use is for candying.

across the valley, divided it into two zones, one flooded with summer lights, the other blue-tinged and cold as a winter landscape.

Since in accordance with the rules of the Carthusian Order the monastery contained exactly thirteen monks, including the Abbot, it had escaped the destruction decreed in 1836 for all religious houses containing less than twelve inmates. But the community had been dissolved, like all the others, and the monastery itself suppressed—that is to say, made over to the State—and the State of Majorca, at a loss how to use these extensive buildings, had decided to let them crumble away, but meanwhile lease the cells to layfolk as residences. Although the rent asked was extremely reasonable, the villagers of Valldemosa had not taken advantage of the offer, perhaps because of their deep piety and the regard they had felt for their monks, perhaps also from superstitious fear: which, though it did not prevent them from coming to dance there on carnival nights, as I shall tell later, made them look askance on our presence within these venerable walls, and find it most disrespectful.

However, the greater part of the monastery is occupied, during the summer heat, by Palma tradespeople who, at this altitude and beneath these thick vaults, expect a fresher air than can be found in the plain or city. But at the onset of winter, cold drives them away, and when we settled there the only other occupants were the apothecary, the sacristan, and Maria Antonia.

Maria Antonia was what you might call a woman of confidence, who had, I believe, escaped from poverty on the mainland, and rented a cell in order to make a living out of the summer visitors. Her cell, which adjoined ours, served as our kitchen, while the lady herself played at being our housekeeper. She had once been handsome, and was still slender and neat; of good family, or so she said; with charming manners, a well-pitched voice and a glib tongue, and a most remarkable brand of hospitality. She would offer her services to new arrivals, but with an outraged air, almost hiding her face in horror, refuse any kind of payment for her trouble. She worked, she used to say, for the love of God, and just to help, with the sole aim of winning the friendship of her neighbours. Her furniture consisted of a trestle-bed, a brazier, two straw-bottomed chairs, a crucifix and a few earthenware dishes. She generously gave you the freedom of all these, and you could set up your cooking-pot and lodge your maid on her premises.

In return she won the freedom of your household, and helped herself to the most respectable of your old clothes and the best things in your larder. I have never seen a pious mouth with a greater relish for delicacies, or fingers nimbler at snatching morsels from the bottom of boiling stews without getting scalded, or a more capacious throat for slily ingurgitating her beloved hosts' sugar and coffee, while continuing to hum a hymn, or a *bolero*. A wholly disinterested spectator would have thought it remarkably amusing to watch this worthy Antonia, with our chambermaid Catalina, the arch-witch[1] of Valldemosa, and the *niña*, a dishevelled little monster who acted as help, all grappling with our dinner together. This took place at the hour of the Angelus, which these three cats never forgot to yowl, in the form of a duet by the two elder ones, as they pillaged every dish—the little one responding *amen* as she filched a chop or comfit with unparalleled dexterity. It was at first well worth pretending not to notice this scene, which cried out for a painter; but when the rains frequently cut our communications with Palma, and food grew scarce, the so-called help of Maria Antonia and her gang became less amusing, and my children and I had to take turns, standing guard over our provisions. I can remember hiding beneath my bolster, almost, a basketful of rusks which were essential for breakfast next morning, and hovering like a vulture above our outdoor stoves to scare away those lesser birds of prey who would have raided our fish-kettle and left us nothing but fish bones.

The sacristan was a hefty young fellow who had once perhaps acted as acolyte for the Carthusians, and since taken charge of the monastery keys. He had a disgraceful record: being guilty in fact and in law of having seduced and got with child a young

[1] This may be literally intended. Valldemosa was once famous for witches, and witches still practised there when I first visited it in 1929; but the tourist trade has driven the cult farther afield.

lady who had spent a few months there with her parents.[1] He pleaded in excuse that the only virgins whom the State had commissioned him to protect were the ones in the monastery paintings. Though not in the least good-looking, he played the dandy: that is to say, instead of the fine, semi-Arab costume worn by other men of his class, he sported European trousers and braces which undoubtedly caught the eye of local beauties. His sister was the loveliest Majorcan girl I have ever seen. They did not live in the monastery, being wealthy and proud and having a house in the village; but went their rounds every day and were cronies of Maria Antonia who, if she did not happen to feel hungry, would often invite them to eat our dinner for her.

The apothecary, an ex-Carthusian monk, would shut himself up in his cell, resume his once-white habit, and chant the offices in solitary state. If a visitor rang at his door to ask for marsh-mallow or couch-grass (the only drugs in stock) he hurriedly threw his habit under the bed and appeared in black breeches, stockings and waistcoat, looking exactly like the operatic characters whom Moliere used to put on the stage in his ballet interludes. Though a very suspicious old man, he never complained of his lot, and if he prayed perhaps for the triumph of Don Carlos and the return of the Holy Office, this did not mean that he would have harmed a fly. He sold us his couch-grass for its weight in gold, and these little profits perhaps helped to console him for his release from the vow of poverty. His cell was away at the entrance of the Charterhouse, in a kind of recess, its door hidden behind a thicket of castor-oil bushes and other luxuriant medicinal plants. Lurking there like an old hare, afraid of setting the dogs on his trail, he rarely made an appearance; and if we had not visited him several times to buy his juleps, we should never have suspected that a Carthusian was still about.[2]

This Charterhouse has no architectural beauties, but is a series of sturdy, amply-designed buildings. Its massive walls of dressed

[1] The result, then as now, would have been that the child went to an orphanage and the mother into a nunnery.

[2] The jars and other furnishings of the apothecary's shop have recently been reassembled by the present owners of the Charterhouse, and are among the earliest in Europe.

stone enclose an area which would have sufficed to house an army corps. Yet the whole edifice had been built for only twelve monks and their prior. The 'new cloisters' alone—at various periods three Carthusian monasteries have here been built on to one another—give access to twelve cells, each consisting of three spacious rooms. At right angles to these cloisters run two lines of chapels, twelve in all; because each monk had his own chapel, where he used to retire for solitary devotion. Each was differently decorated, with gilt and pictures in the most vulgar taste, and the plastered saints in coloured wood were so frightful that I, for one, should not have cared to meet them out of their niches after dark. These oratories had been paved with glazed earthenware tiles, very effectively arranged in mosaic patterns. Here the Moorish style still prevails, the only good style to have become traditional in Majorca. Finally, each of the chapels is equipped with a cistern, or a conch in fine local marble, the Carthusian having been bound to wash his oratory every day. Such coolness prevails in these dark, vaulted rooms, with their glazed floors, as might well, under the scorching heat of the Dog-star, have converted the long hours of prayer into a kind of sensual pleasure.

The fourth side of the New Cloister, the middle of which is occupied by a courtyard symmetrically planted with box-trees —they had not yet outgrown the pyramidal shapes forced on them by the monks' shears—runs behind a lovely church, its coolness and cleanliness contrasting pleasantly with the neglect and emptiness of the monastery. We hoped to find an organ there, forgetting that the Carthusian Rule bans all musical instruments as being a vain and luxurious indulgence of the senses. This church consists of a single nave; earthenware tiles, exquisitely painted with bunches of flowers and forming a carpet-like pattern, pave it. The panelled wainscoting, confessionals and doors are of simple design; but the faultlessness of their fillets, and the cleanness and restraint of the decorative work, testify to a skilled craftsmanship no longer found even among French cabinetmakers, and unfortunately a lost art in Majorca, too. M. Tastu told me that in the whole island two carpenters alone still keep their trade on the level of an art. The carpenter whom we employed at Valldemosa was certainly an artist, though only as regards music and painting. He came into our cell one day to put up some deal shelves, and inspected all our artistic impedimenta with the same ingenuous and prying curiosity that I had once observed among the Slavonic Greeks. He was a little shocked by the sketches which my son had based on some Goya drawings of a monastic orgy and hung on the walls of our cell; but catching sight of an engraving—Rubens's *Descent from the Cross*—he stood for a long time in a strange contemplation. Asked what his thoughts were, he replied in his dialect: 'There is nothing so beautiful or so natural in all Majorca.'

The word 'natural' spoken by a peasant with the mane and manners of a savage impressed us greatly. The sound of piano playing threw him into a rapture. He would leave his work, to come and stand behind the pianist's chair, with mouth half-open and eyes bulging. These exalted instincts, however, did not prevent him from being a thief, like all Majorcan peasants in their dealings with foreigners, when they are entirely without conscience, although said to be scrupulously honest one with another.[1] He charged us a fabulous sum, and stretched greedy hands for all the small goods of French manufacture which we had brought to use ourselves. It was with difficulty that I rescued my toilet accessories from his capacious pockets. What tempted him most was a cut-glass tumbler, or perhaps the toothbrush which stood in it, although he certainly did not understand its use. This man combined the artistic yearning of an Italian with the rapacious instincts of a Malay or Kaffir.

I have not digressed so far as to forget the one object of artistic value that we found in the Charterhouse. This was a polychrome wooden image of St. Bruno,[2] standing in the church, and remarkably well-designed. The hands, excellently studied, were raised in devout and heart-rending invocation; the face wore a most sublime expression of faith under suffering. And yet this was the work of an ignorant man, because the image set opposite to

[1] Nowadays it is rather the foreigners who bilk the Majorcans, not the Majorcans who defraud the foreigners; in a village, anyone losing his reputation for honesty either towards his neighbours or towards visitors, is politely shunned and usually moves away.

[2] Founder of the Carthusian Order.

it, and carved by the same person, was altogether wretched. In creating St. Bruno, he must have had a flash of inspiration, an exalted religious impulse which raised him above himself. I doubt whether the saintly zealot of Grenoble has ever before been portrayed with such deep and passionate understanding: this was the personification of Christian asceticism. Yet, in Majorca, the symbol of that bygone philosophy stood neglected.

One enters the New Cloister through the old; the two are connected by a very simple turning which my defective topographical memory[1] would never allow me to recognize until I had lost myself in the third cloister. This part of the building, which I ought to call the first cloister, as being the oldest, is also the smallest. It looks delightful. The courtyard encircled by its broken walls was the monks' cemetery. No inscription marks the graves that these Carthusians used to dig for themselves while still alive, and where nothing might dispute death's claim to annihilate their memory. The only indication of the tombs are slight swellings above the turf. M. Laurens has recalled the appearance of this cloister in a lovely drawing; I recognize with indescribable pleasure the little well with pointed gable, the stone window-crosses festooned by all the weeds that wander over ruins, and the tall, upright cypresses standing at night like black spectres around the white wooden cross. I am sorry that he missed seeing the moon rise behind the beautiful mountain of amber-coloured sandstone which towers above this cloister, and that he has left out of the foreground an old laurel-tree with huge trunk and withered crown; perhaps it was no longer extant when he visited the Charterhouse. But I recognized both in his drawing and his text an honourable mention of the lovely dwarf palm-tree (*chamoerops*), perhaps one of the sturdiest of its species in Europe, which I protected from my children's botanical zeal.

Around this cloister stand fifteenth-century Carthusian chapels; they are hermetically sealed and the sacristan would not open them for anyone. This greatly excited our curiosity, but by peering through chinks, in the course of our walks, we thought that

[1] A plan of the monastery, made soon after its dissolution, shows her description of it to have been wrong in almost every particular.

we could make out the remains of beautiful furniture and antique wooden carvings. Many valuable objects might well be hidden in these mysterious glory-holes from which nobody in Majorca will ever bother to shake off the dust.

The second cloister contains another twelve cells and twelve chapels. Its decaying arches have great character. They no longer hold anything up, and when passing through them at evening, in rough weather, we would commend our souls to God; because every storm that passed over the monastery blew down another piece of the wall, or another stone from the arches. Never have I heard the wind howl so desperately as in these hollow, echoing galleries. The noise of the torrents, the clouds scudding past, the loud monotonous roar of the sea interrupted by the whistling of the storm, and the mournful cries of the seagulls as they swept past, startled and blown off course by the blustering wind; then great mists which fell suddenly like a shroud[1] and which, seeping into the cloister through the shattered arches, made us invisible and turned the little lamp we carried to guide us into a wandering will o' the wisp—these, and a thousand other details of this cœnobitic life that crowd together in my memory, all combined to make our monastery the most romantic dwelling place in the world.

I was not sorry for once to see in full and actual detail what I had hitherto seen only in dreams, or in fashionable ballads, or during the Nuns' Act in *Robert the Devil*, at the Opera. We even had our weird spectres, which I shall presently describe; and all this romanticism posing realistically before my eyes did not fail to inspire me with certain thoughts on romanticism in general.

To the mass of buildings already described, must be added the prior's quarters which, like many other mysterious recesses, we were unable to view; also the cells of the lay brothers; a little church belonging to the old Charterhouse; several annexes intended for distinguished personages who went into retreat there or fulfilled penitentiary devotions; and certain small courtyards surrounded by stables for the community's livestock; accommodation for the numerous retinue of visitors; in fact, a

[1] Valldemosa is constantly at cloud level and, except during the summer heats, has the worst weather of any village in the island.

complete phalanstery,[1] as we would say today, under the protection of the Virgin and St. Bruno.

When the weather did not permit us to climb the mountain, we would take our walks under cover in the monastery, and the exploration of this enormous manor used to occupy us for hours on end. Something within these deserted walls appealed to my curiosity and urged me to probe the inner secret of monastic life. Its traces were so fresh that I often thought I could hear the shuffle of sandals along the paved walk and the murmur of prayer beneath the chapel vaults. We might still read Latin prayers printed and stuck on the walls of our cells, even in secret nooks where I should never have imagined anyone would go to say his *oremus.*

Once, while on an expedition to explore the upper storeys, we stumbled on a lovely gallery, from which we could look down into a large, beautiful chapel, completely furnished and in such good order that it might have been abandoned only the day before. The prior's chair was still in its place, and the programme of the week's religious exercises, pinned to a black wooden frame, hung from an arch in the middle of the chapter stalls. Each stall had a small holy image stuck on the back, probably the patron saint of the monk who once occupied it. The smell of incense in which the walls had for so long been steeped, lingered faintly yet. Withered flowers decked the altars, and half-burned candles were still ranked in their sconces. The undisturbed decorum that reigned here contrasted strangely with the ruins outside, the tall brambles which overgrew the windows, and the shouts of naughty boys playing duckstone in the cloisters with pieces of mosaic.

As for my children, their passionate love of the marvellous made them even more eager than myself to indulge in this lively game of discovery. My daughter certainly expected to find a fairy palace full of wonders in the monastery attics, and my son hoped to unearth from the debris the relics of some strange and awful tragedy. I was often alarmed to see them climbing like cats over warped planks and across quaking balconies; and

[1] A socialized community in Fourier's ideal scheme, built to accommodate a phalanx, or *falange,* of 1,000 persons.

when, keeping a few steps ahead of me, they vanished around the turn of a winding staircase, I used to imagine that they were lost, and quickened my pace with a dread in which superstition very likely played a part.

Why attempt to deny that sinister abodes like these, dedicated to an even more sinister religious cult, have some effect on the imagination? I would challenge the calmest and coolest brain to preserve perfect sanity here over a long period. Although little fanciful fears, if I may call them so, do not lack a certain charm, they are real enough to call for an effort of self-discipline in overcoming them. I confess that I seldom walked through the cloister after dusk without a feeling of mingled distress and pleasure, which I did not wish to betray for fear of communicating it to my children. Yet they appeared quite insensitive to the atmosphere, and would run gladly in the moonlight under broken arches that seemed to be summoning witches to their Sabbath merry-making. I led them through the cemetery about midnight on several occasions.

However, I forbade them to go out alone in the dark after our first meeting with a tall old man who used to haunt the dark cloisters. He was a former servant or dependant of the community, whose brain often gave way under the combined assaults of wine and religious enthusiasm. He would come wandering drunkenly along, knocking at the doors of the empty cells with a great pilgrim's staff, from which hung a long rosary, summoning the monks in vinous language and praying lugubriously before the chapels. Since he could see a faint light beneath the door of our cell, it was here especially that he came to prowl, uttering threats and fearful curses. He used to visit Maria Antonia, who was terrified by him, and preach her lengthy sermons punctuated by shameless oaths. Then he would settle beside her charcoal brazier, until the sacristan came to remove him by means of compliments and stratagems; for the sacristan was something of a coward, and feared to antagonize him. The old man would afterwards come beating on our door at all hours of the night, and when he grew tired of calling in vain for Father Nicolás, who was his obsession, would sink down at the foot of the Madonna that stood in a niche a few steps from our door, and go to sleep there, a naked knife in one hand and his beads in the other.

We were not greatly alarmed by the uproar this wild animal made, because he could never fall upon people unawares. His approach was heralded from afar by broken exclamations and the sound of his staff on the flagstones, and we had time to beat a retreat. The double door of solid oak which protected our cell could have withstood a far more formidable siege; but we had a prostrate invalid, and these persistent onslaughts, threatening his few hours of rest, were not always amusing. We endured it nevertheless with *mucha calma*, because the local police would certainly not have given us any protection; the fact being that we did not attend mass, whereas our enemy was a holy man who never missed a single service.

One evening we were roused by a visitation of a different order, which I shall never forget. It began with an unaccountable noise comparable only to that of thousands of walnut sacks rolling incessantly over the floor. We hurried out into the cloister, to see what it could be. The cloister was empty and dark as usual; but the noise came nearer and nearer, and soon a faint light began to illuminate the immense depths of the vaults. Gradually it was revealed as the flame of several torches and then, in the ruddy smoke which they emitted, appeared a battalion of beings hateful to God and men. They were no less than Lucifer himself, attended by his whole court; an Archdevil, all in black, horned, with blood-red face, and around him a swarm of imps with birds' heads, horses' tails, and tawdry finery of every colour; also she-devils, or shepherdesses, dressed in white and pink, who looked as if they had been carried off by these unprepossessing devilkins. After the confession already recorded above, I need not deny that for a minute or two, even when I had grasped what was afoot, it called for an effort of will to hold my lamp up steadily in view of this ugly masquerade, lent a truly supernatural look by the hour, the place and the torchlight.

They were only village people, wealthy farmers and tradesmen, celebrating Shrove Tuesday and come to perform their country dance in Maria Antonia's cell. The strange noise attending their progress was made by wooden castanets which several urchins, their faces covered by grimy, hideous masks, were all playing simultaneously, not in regular rhythmic phrases, as in Spain, but in an unbroken rattle like drums beating a double-flam. This noise, which also accompanies their dances, is so crude and harsh that it needs courage to support a quarter of an hour of it. In their festival processions, they break it off suddenly, to sing a *coplita* in unison on a musical phrase that always repeats itself and seems to have no end; then the castanets take up their rattle again, for three or four minutes, splitting everyone's eardrums. There could be no more uncivilized way of celebrating a festival. But the musical phrase, though nothing in itself, takes on great character when thus sung at long intervals, and by voices that have a peculiar quality of being, as it were, veiled even when full-throated, and dragging even when brisk.

I believe that the Moors used to sing like this, and M. Tastu's investigations persuaded him that the chief rhythms and favourite grace-notes of the Majorcans, their whole style in fact, is of Moorish tradition.[1] When we were sailing from Barcelona to Palma, on a warm, dark night illuminated only by the remarkable phosphorescence of the ship's wash, everyone on board was asleep except ourselves and the man at the wheel who, to prevent himself from following suit, sang all night long, but in so soft and restrained a voice that one might have thought him either afraid of waking the watch, or half-asleep himself. We did not weary of listening to his strange song. The rhythm and modulations were altogether different from any music known to us; he seemed to let his voice wander at random, like the smoke from the ship's funnel carried away and rocked by the breeze. It was a reverie rather than a song, a listless wandering of the voice in which conscious thought played little part, that accompanied the rolling of the ship and the hiss of water under the paddles; and though suggesting a vague improvization, was nevertheless confined within a gentle, monotonous pattern.

This contemplative singing was really delightful.

When all these devils reached our door, they crowded around

[1] Jewish and Byzantine influences must not be excluded.

us with great friendliness and courtesy; for, generally speaking, Majorcan manners are by no means fierce or aggressive. King Beelzebub was pleased to address me in Spanish, and reveal himself as a lawyer.[1] Then, to give me a still more exalted idea of himself, he tried French; and, wanting to enquire whether I was enjoying my stay in the Charterhouse, he translated the Spanish word *cartuja* by the French *cartouche*, cartridge, which of course involved us in a slight misunderstanding. But the Majorcan Devil is not obliged to speak every language.

Their dances are gayer than the songs. We followed them into Maria Antonia's cell, across which curved sprays of ivy hung with little paper lanterns. The orchestra, consisting of a guitar, a mandoline, a treble violin and three or four pairs of castanets, began to play the native *jotas* and *fandangos*, like those of Spain, but of more original rhythm and bolder pattern.

This festival honoured Rafael Torres, a wealthy tenant-farmer of Valldemosa, who had married a quite pretty girl a few days before. The new husband was condemned to approach each of the women in turn and dance in front of her, which occupied most of the evening. No other man took the floor at all. During these performances the whole gathering, including the mayor himself, with his monk's cowl and his great black, silver-headed staff, squatted solemnly and silently on the floor in the Oriental or African style.[2]

The Majorcan *boleros* have an ancestral gravity, and none of the secular charm that one admires in Andalusia. Men and women keep their arms spread out and still, while their fingers rattle the castanets without pause. The handsome Rafael danced dutifully until he had finished his stint, and then went to crouch down with the others, whereupon the local devils had their hour of glory. One young lad, slim-waisted as a wasp, aroused general admiration by the stiffness of his movements, and by his galvanic jumps, never shifting his position or allowing the least spark of merriment to light up his face. A hefty labourer,

[1] His name was Jaime Prohens.

[2] Maurice Sand's sketch of this occasion shows everyone, including the mayor, seated on chairs; except for one man who has chosen a heap of sacks, and seven standing figures.

who seemed to fancy himself as a lady-killer, tried to leg it with folded arms in the Spanish fashion, but was jeered at, as he richly deserved, for his was the most absurd caricature imaginable. These country dances would have kept us enthralled for a long time, had it not been for the smell of rancid oil and garlic which the ladies and gentlemen exuded, and which literally caught at one's throat.

We were less interested in the carnival disguises than in the traditional Majorcan holiday costumes. These are elegant and graceful. The women wear the *rebozillo*, a white wimple made of lace or muslin, and consisting of two parts: one, the *rebozillo en amunt*, fixed rather towards the back of the head, and passing underneath the chin like a nun's coif: and the other, the *rebozillo en volant*, flowing loosely like a cape over the shoulders. Their hair is neatly parted in the middle, and caught behind in a long thick plait that emerges from the *rebozillo* and is tucked into the belt at one side. On ordinary days of labour, however, the hair is left unplaited and hangs down the back in the *estufada*, which means loose array. The bodice, made of merino or black silk, low necked, with short sleeves, is adorned, above the elbow and on the back-seams, with jewelled buttons through which silver chains are stylishly threaded. These women have slender, well-proportioned figures, and tiny feet which, on holidays, are elegantly shod. Every village girl wears open-work linen stockings, satin shoes, a gold chain around the neck,[1] and several yards of silver chains to hang around her corsage and dangle at her belt. I saw many Majorcan girls with beautiful bodies, few with beautiful faces; but their features, while as regular as those seen in Andalusia, wear a franker and gentler expression. The Sóller district, which I did not visit, enjoys a great reputation for female beauty.[2]

The men whom I saw were not handsome, but all seemed so at first sight because of their becoming costume. This consists, on Sundays and holidays, of a *gipó*, or waistcoat, cut heart-shape

[1] Gold chains, coins and brooches were called in and melted down during the recent Civil War.

[2] The girls of the mountains are, on the whole, far better looking than those of the plain; as can be seen in the autumn, when gangs of olive-pickers come up to Valldemosa and Deyá to help with the harvest.

from some flowered material, and worn wide open, as is also the *sayo*, a short, close-fitting, buttonless black jacket, like a woman's bodice. A resplendently white shirt, caught at the neck and sleeves by embroidered bands, leaves the throat bare and the chest gleaming with fine linen: which always sets off a costume to great advantage. A coloured sash is tied tightly around the waist, over wide, baggy, Turkish pantaloons made from striped cotton or silk of local manufacture; below come white, black, or fawn linen stockings and shoes of undressed, natural-coloured calf-skin. The wide-brimmed hat, made of *moxine*, or wild-cat's fur, with cords and tassels of silk and gold thread, detracts from the Oriental character of this attire. At home, they tie a silk scarf or a printed calico handkerchief, turban-wise round their heads, which suits them much better. In winter they often wear a black woollen skull-cap over their tonsure, for they shave the crown of their head like priests, whether as a measure of cleanliness—and Heaven knows it does not get them very far!—or whether for religious reasons, I cannot say. Their thick, coarse, frizzy manes flow (in so far as a mane can be said to flow) around their necks. A fringe cut across the forehead completes this mediæval hair style and gives every face a vigorous look.

In the fields, their costume is less formal, but still more picturesque. Their legs are bare, or cased as far as the knees in tan leather gaiters, according to the season. In hot weather, they wear only a shirt and pantaloons.[1] In winter they wrap themselves in a grey cloak which suggests a monk's habit, or in a huge African goat's skin, with the hair outside. When they pass in groups, wearing these long fawn-coloured skins, which have a black streak down the spine, they look from the rear just like a herd of goats balancing on their hind legs. Nearly always, when they go out to the fields or come home again, one of them walks ahead playing a guitar or a flute,[2] and the others follow silently at his heels, hanging their heads with a look of

1 The shirt is left hanging free for coolness

2 Only shepherds in remote districts now play the flute, or the bagpipe, which is of the Norwich, not the Highland, type. Guitars are rarely heard, except in the towns.

complete guilelessness and stupidity, though by no means lacking in shrewdness. Nobody but a complete fool would be deceived by their appearance.

They are usually tall, and their costume lends an effect of slenderness, which makes them seem taller still. The neck, always uncovered, is fine and strong; the chest, unconfined by tight waistcoats and braces, is open and well-developed; but almost every man has bandy legs.

It was our impression that the features of the older men, if not handsome, were at least serious and bore a certain stamp of nobility. They all looked like monks, whereas the younger generation seemed of a vulgar and more lusty type: as it were a sudden break in the male line of descent. Can it be only twenty years since the monks ceased to interfere with the privacy of the home?[1]

[1] In October 1809, Sir John Carr, an English barrister, had visited the Charterhouse and described it as follows:

'When we entered upon the estates of the convent, the hand of culture seemed to have been still more actively and skilfully employed. After winding along the sides of the most picturesque hills, richly clothed to their summits, belted with ridges or terrace-walls rising above each other, kept in the greatest order, and by vines, entwined round almond-trees bending with rich and ponderous clusters, we discerned the pale yellow front of the monastery seated midway on the side of a mountain in a calm and majestic retreat, deriving a sort of sylvan solemnity from groups of cypresses, palms, and poplars, and interminable woods of olives. . .

'As we approached the monastery, we met several of the holy brethren taking their afternoon walk. We brought provisions and a cook with us, which are very necessary, as the monks never suffer meat, unless brought by strangers, to enter their walls; and their funds were at this time rather at a low ebb on account of the erection of a noble church adjoining the convent, which as far as it had proceeded, had dipped deeply into their treasury. Owing to this heavy expenditure, they had given notice in the Palma *Gazette* that, with an exception of the English, they could not entertain strangers till their new church was finished.

'The superior, an enormous and jolly old man, paid us the compliment of rising from his siesta to receive us, and whilst our dinner was preparing, one of the monks, a very intelligent man, conducted us over the convent and church. The latter is a vast and noble pile, the internal decorations of which were not half finished. The dome and roof were painted in gaudy colours and bad taste by an Italian artist, and the bases of the pilasters were formed of fine marble from the neighbouring rocks. There was a colossal figure of the Virgin holding a *silesio*, a net of iron with sharp points, which is by way of penance fastened round the thigh, or loins of female penitents, finely executed in wood, intended for one of the lateral chapels of the church. The number of monks was twenty-nine, of whom seventeen had fled from Barcelona. Their cells were handsome apartments. The gardens of the convent are spacious; in some of them we saw land-tortoises. From a long terrace under arches of vines, there is a superb view of the surrounding valleys and mountains. After an excellent repast, we took leave of our prior, who expressed himself warmly attached to the English, and talked much of an entertainment which had been given to him, on board of an English frigate, and on our way to our mules, which were left in the village of Valldemosa, we were taken to the church, in which we saw nothing worthy of notice, but the levity with which the attendant monk evidently treated the mummery which he showed us.'

George Sand's suggestion that the Valldemosans were monks' bastards she explained later as 'just a traveller's joke'.

Of her relations with the village, Charles Dombowski, who visited the cell on January 15th, 1839, wrote in his travel book:

'The most famous novelist of our day, George Sand, lives a retired life in a cell of the ancient Carthusian monastery in Valldemosa. The day that I arrived the village was celebrating the feast of St. Anthony, who is the patron saint of Majorca. A priest stood in the porch of the town hall, sprinkling holy water over the long procession of pigs and mules which came filing past a statue of the saint. Peasants, masked in honour of the carnival, led these beasts, and at the moment of the blessing placed an offering for the saint into a silver dish held by a young cleric. When the religious part of the ceremony was over, the villagers lit their lanterns as a sign of their rejoicing, and congregated in the village inn to dance the *fandango mallorquin*. Being the bearer of a bundle of letters and newspapers for George Sand, I left these gay people to go and fulfil my commission to the fair anchorite. She received me with all that courtesy and charming simplicity which one might expect from what one knows of her, and begged me to stay to dinner in order to repay me—as she put it—the postage on her mail.

'That evening I went back to the inn, where they were still dancing. The mayor and parish priest of the village were there, amongst the spectators, and had already heard of my visit to the new solitary who dwelt in the Cartuja. You cannot imagine how hurt these people were that George Sand had not condescended to attend the morning's ceremony. The priest who had been so generous with his holy water was highly mortified. '*Por cierto*,' he said to me, '*que esta señora francesa tiene que ser una mujer muy particular*'—'This French lady must indeed be a strange person! Just think of it: she never speaks to a living soul, never leaves the Cartuja, and never shows her face in church, not even on Sundays, and goodness knows how many mortal sins she is amassing! Furthermore, I have it from the apothecary, who also lives in the Cartuja, that *la señora* makes cigarettes like nothing on earth, drinks coffee at all hours, sleeps by day, and does nothing but smoke and write all night. I beg you, dear sir, since you know her, to tell us what she has come to do here in midwinter.' The parish priest's outburst may give you some idea of the impression which George Sand's arrival has created in Majorca. I do not think that it would be any exaggeration to say that nothing has made such a sensation since the Carlist rising of 1835, which was led—poor devil—by the bellringer of the town of Manacor, who paid for it with his head.'

Chapter Fourteen

I WRITE above that I tried to detect the secret of monastic life in places where its marks were still fresh. Not that I expected to discover historical mysteries associated with this particular Charterhouse; I only asked its deserted walls to disclose the inner thoughts of the silent recluses whom they had, for centuries, debarred from the life of their fellow-humans. I should have liked to follow the frayed or broken thread of Christian faith in the souls which each generation cast there, sacrificing them to a jealous God whose need for human victims was as great as that of the pagan idols He displaced. I should, in fact, have liked to revivify one dead Carthusian from the fifteenth century and one from the nineteenth, and compare the two—both Catholics, but unexpectedly a world apart in faith—asking each what he thought of the other.

It seemed easy enough to construct a plausible interpretation of the mediæval monk's life. I saw him as a simple Christian, ardent, sincere, heartbroken at the spectacle provided by the wars, dissensions and sufferings of his contemporaries, fleeing from that abyss of evils to withdraw and separate himself as far as possible in ascetic meditation from a life where the perfectibility of the masses was a concept eluding the comprehension of the individual. But the nineteenth-century Carthusian, the last monk to occupy the cell I had rented, closing his eyes to the now perceptible and manifest progress of humanity, unconcerned by the lives of his contemporaries, no longer understanding religion, the Pope, the Church, society, or himself, and no longer seeing anything in the Charterhouse but a safe, roomy, pleasant residence, or anything in his vocation but an opportunity to indulge his instincts with impunity, and a means of winning, unearned by merit, the respectful esteem of devout peasants and women—I found him far harder to evoke. I was at a loss to estimate with any conviction what degree of self-reproach, blindness, hypocrisy, or insincerity he must have attained. Unless he was devoid of all intelligence, he could not possibly have had real faith in the Roman Church. Nor could he have been a confirmed atheist, for then his whole life would have been a repulsive lie, and I refuse to believe that men can be either wholly stupid or wholly base. It was the idea of this monk's conflicts—the choice which confronted him between rebellion and submission, between philosophical doubt and superstitious dread—that rose like a hell before my eyes; and the more I thought about it, the more heavily did the sufferings and perturbations I ascribed to him weigh on my inflamed fancy. The increasing need for comfort, hygiene, and even elegance, that had crept into the life of these recluses, could be seen by a casual glance from the old cloisters to the new; equally evident was the slackening of austerity, and the diminishment of mortification and penitence. Whereas all the old cells had been dark, cramped and draughty, the new ones were bright, airy, and well built. Yet a description of our cell will give an idea how strict the Carthusian rule was, even when evaded and mitigated as much as possible.

Imagine three large, gracefully arched rooms, ventilated at the base by rosettes—no two alike and of a very graceful design—cut through the yard-thick wall to the outside air. These rooms are separated from the cloister by a dark entry, and closed by a stout oak door. The middle room is intended for reading, prayer and contemplation; its only piece of furniture, a large combined praying-desk and grandfather-chair, six or eight feet tall, has been fixed firmly in the wall. The bedroom lies on the right; facing the entry, in a very low recess, stands the bed, with stone slabs piled above it in sepulchral style. On the left, the workshop, dining room and store room. At the far end, the larder, the wooden hatch of which communicates with the cloister; and through this the monk's food was passed in to him. His kitchen consisted of two small stoves placed outside the cell, though no longer in the open air as the strict rule had enjoined. An arched porch, giving access to the garden, sheltered his culinary operations from the weather, and allowed him to devote rather more time to this pursuit than the founder can have wished. Also, the introduction of a fireplace into the dining room proclaimed many other relaxations, although the architect had not been skilful enough to design a chimney that drew.

Along the back of the cell, level with the rosettes, ran a long, narrow, dark tunnel, intended to ventilate it, and a loft above had been used for storing maize, onions, beans and other frugal winter stores. At the front, facing south, the three rooms opened on a small garden which occupied exactly as much space as they did. This pleasance, divided from its neighbour by ten-foot walls, rested on a solidly-built terrace, and overlooked the orange grove that spread from one end to the other of the mountain tier immediately below. The tier below that was occupied by a fine grape arbour, the next tier by almonds and palms, and so on, down to the bottom of the valley which, as I have already said, seemed one huge garden.

The right side of each monk's private plot was occupied by a tank of dressed stone, three or four feet wide by as many deep, designed to receive the mountain waters from courses cut in the terrace balustrade. They were conveyed to the plot by stone channels, which formed a cross dividing it into four equal squares. I could never make out why such an extravagant amount of water should be needed to quench the thirst of one solitary man and irrigate four ten-foot-square flower beds. Were it not that an abhorrence of bathing is a well-known characteristic of Catholic monks, and that even the Majorcan laymen are habitually abstemious in this respect,[1] these worthy Carthusians might have been supposed to spend their whole lives washing themselves like Indian priests.

This pleasance, then, with its pomegranate, lemon and orange trees, and its raised brick paths, which were shaded like the tank by fragrant arbours, resembled an elegant drawing-room full of

[1] They are an extremely clean people, change their linen frequently, and despise the French as dirty.

flowers and greenery. Here the monk could walk dry-shod on wet days; revive his lawn with a sheet of running water during scorching heat; stand on the edge of a splendid terrace and inhale the fragrance of the oranges, whose bushy tops put forth glittering domes of flowers and fruit beneath his eyes; and gaze in complete tranquillity at the landscape—a combination, as I have already remarked, of severity and grace, melancholy and magnificence. Finally, he could grow rare and precious flowers to feast his eyes, gather the most luscious fruit to quench his thirst, listen to the sea's sublime murmur, gaze at the glory of a summer night beneath a perfect sky, and worship the Eternal God in the most beautiful temple which He has ever opened to man in the heart of Nature. Such seemed to me, at first, the ineffable delights of the Carthusians; and such delights I promised myself, as I settled into one of their cells. All seemed arranged to satisfy the splendid imaginative fancies or dreams of a picked force of poets and artists.

But when one pictures the life of a man who lacks intelligence and hence the power to dream or meditate, who has no faith, perhaps—that is to say, no rapture and no contemplation—when one thinks of him immured within this cell whose solid walls can neither hear nor answer him, indurated by the hardships of the Rule and forced to observe its letter without understanding the spirit, destined to the horror of isolation, forced to content himself with distant glimpses, from this mountain height, of mankind crawling along the valley-floor; a perpetual stranger to a few other souls imprisoned beside him, vowed to the selfsame silence,[1] buried in the same tomb, always close yet always apart, even in prayer—finally, when one feels one's own self, a free and rational being, sympathetically drawn into certain fears and certain failings, the whole surroundings assume the dark shadows that shroud a life of emptiness, error and impotence.

It is then easy to understand the immeasurable boredom of

[1] The Rule allowed a weekly half-hour of general conversation, besides confessions and communal devotions. Any important message that could not be conveyed by gestures was spelled out with pegs, pushed into alphabetically marked holes on a wooden board—still shown in the Church sacristy.

the monk on whom Nature lavishes her loveliest display, but who takes small pleasure in it, because he has no companion with whom to share his enjoyment; the brutish gloom of the penitent who, animal-like, no longer suffers from anything except extremes of cold and heat; and the deadly chill of the Christian in whom nothing can revive or quicken the spirit of asceticism. Doomed to eat alone, work alone, suffer and pray alone, he must surely have had only one need left, namely, to escape from this dreadful confinement; and I was told that the last Carthusians loved it so little that some of them stayed away for weeks and months on end, and their superior was powerless to recall them.

I am much afraid my lengthy and detailed description of our Charterhouse has not conveyed the least notion of the magic that it once exercised on us—of the romantic glamour which wore off so soon on closer examination. As usual, I have given way to the influence of memories and now, after this attempt to convey my impressions, I wonder why I could not have said in twenty lines what has already covered as many pages: simply, that peace of mind and freedom from care, with everything that includes these, seem delightful at first to a weary spirit, but one more glance and the spell is broken. The truth is that only genius can draw a complete and vivid picture with a single stroke of the brush. When M. Lamennais once visited the *camaldules* at Tivoli, he was overcome by the same feeling, and expressed it with masterly conciseness:

'We reached the monks' retreat,' he wrote in his *Affaires de Rome*, 'at the hour of communal prayer. All seemed to us fairly advanced in age, and taller than the average. After the office they remained kneeling, motionless, deep in meditation, forming two rows along one side of the nave. They seemed no longer of this earth; their shaven heads bowed beneath other thoughts and other preoccupations than ours; giving no outward sign of life; wrapped in their long white cloaks, like the praying statues of old tombs. We can well understand the kind of attraction exerted by this solitary life on certain world-weary, disillusioned spirits. Who has not aspired to something of the sort? Who has not turned his eyes more than once towards the desert of solitude, dreaming that he will find peace in a forest nook or mountain grotto, near a secret spring where only the birds of the air slake their thirst? But such is not the true destiny of man: man is born for action and has an appointed task to fulfil. What matter, if it be hard? Is he not faced with the task of Love?'

Having always been impressed by this brief paragraph, packed with vivid phrases, lofty aspirations, profound ideas and reflections, which is interjected, as if accidentally, in the middle of M. Lamennais's account of his experiences at the Holy See, I am sure that eventually some great painter will make it the subject of a picture. On one side, the *camaldules* at their prayers, humble, pacific monks, for ever useless, for ever powerless, bowed ghosts, the last exemplars of a worship about to be swallowed up in the darkness of the past, and no less cold and cheerless than the tomb-stones beneath their knees; on the other, the man of the future, the last priest, quickened by the Church's final spark of genius, pondering on the fate of these monks, observing them with an artist's eye, judging them philosophically. Here, the Levites of Death motionless under their shrouds, there, the Apostle of Life, journeying unwearied through the boundless fields of thought, already bidding a last friendly farewell to the poetry of the cloister, and shaking the dust of the Papal city from his feet, to stride forward along the blessed road of moral freedom.

I have not been able to garner any historical facts about our Charterhouse, except a sermon preached by St. Vincent Ferrier at Valldemosa, and here again I am indebted to M. Tastu for the correct account. This sermon became for the Majorcans the great event of the year 1413, and it is interesting to learn how eagerly a missionary could be welcomed at that time, and with what solemn ceremony he was entertained.

> As early as the year 1409, the Majorcans, meeting in a great assembly, resolved that a letter should be sent to Master Vincent Ferrer, or Ferrier, inviting him to come and preach in Majorca. It was Don Luis de Prades, Bishop of Majorca, Cardinal *camerlingo* of Pope Benedict XIII, (the Anti-pope Peter de Luna) who, in 1412, wrote a letter to the aldermen

of Valencia beseeching the apostolic aid of Master Vincent and who, in the following year, embarked with him at Barcelona and set sail for Palma. On the very day after his arrival, the saintly missionary began his sermons and organized nocturnal processions. The island was suffering from a most severe drought, but rain began to fall at Master Vincent's third sermon. This is how these particulars were reported to King Ferdinand by his Royal Procurator, Don Pedro de Casaldaguila:

'Most High, Most Excellent Prince and Victorious Lord:

'I have the honour of communicating to you that Master Vincent arrived in this City on the first day of September, being welcomed here with due solemnity. On Saturday morning he preached to a vast throng, who heard him with such devotion that now every night processions are held in which men, women and children may be seen scourging themselves. And since no rain had fallen for a long time, the Lord God, moved by the prayers of the children and the people, was pleased that, after he had preached his third sermon, this Realm, which was dying of drought, should see fall an abundant rain throughout the island, whereat the inhabitants rejoiced greatly.

'May Our Lord God succour you for many years, Most Victorious Lord, and exalt your Royal Crown!

'Majorca, September 11th, 1413.'

Such an ever-increasing crowd of believers flocked to hear the holy missionary that they could not be accommodated in the huge church of St. Dominic, and the extensive monastery garden had to be made over to them, by setting up stands and pulling down walls.

St. Vincent Ferrier continued to preach in Palma until October 3rd, when he left for a tour of the island. His first halt was at Valldemosa, in the monastery which was to welcome and house him, and which he doubtless chose out of regard for his brother Boniface, then General of the Carthusian Order. The prior of Valldemosa had come to fetch him from Palma. At Valldemosa, the church was even less capable of containing the eager throng. A chronicler records:

'The town of Valldemosa treasures the memory of the time when St. Vincent Ferrier came here to sow the word of God. Within the bounds of the said town lies an estate named Son Gual; thither the missionary repaired, followed by a countless multitude. It was a wide, level field; his pulpit being the hollow trunk of a huge and ancient olive-tree. A heavy shower of rain threatened. It seemed that the Devil, the author of winds, lightning and thunder, was tempting the congregation to disperse and take shelter, which some of them were already doing, when St. Vincent ordered them to stay their ground, and began to pray; whereupon a cloud at once spread like a canopy over him and his hearers; yet those who had continued to work in a neighbouring field perforce abandoned their labours.

'The ancient tree-trunk was still in existence less than a century ago; for our forefathers had preserved it with scrupulous care. Later, the heirs to the Son Gual estate having neglected to care for this sacred relic, its history was forgotten. But God had not willed that St. Vincent's rough pulpit should be lost to human memory. Some servants of the estate, going out to gather wood, caught sight of the tree and set themselves to hew it in pieces, but their axes immediately broke; and when news of this reached the ears of the older inhabitants, the cry 'A Miracle!' went up, and the sacred olive-tree was spared. Later it came to pass that this tree split into thirty-four pieces; and, although close to the town, no one dared touch them.'

To return to the holy preacher: he carried the word of God to the smallest hamlets of the island, healing the sick in body and in spirit. The water of a spring which rises near Valldemosa was the only medicament he prescribed. This spring still goes by the name of *Sa Bassa Ferrara*, or 'Ferrer's Pool'. St. Vincent spent six months in the island, and was then recalled by King Ferdinand of Aragon, to

> help him repair the schism which was afflicting the West. The saint took leave of the Majorcans on February 22nd, 1414, in Palma Cathedral and, having blessed the congregation, he went aboard his ship, escorted by the jurors, the noblemen, and a great horde of common people, performing many miracles on the way; as the chroniclers record, and as the tradition still endures in the Balearic islands.

This account, which would bring a smile to the lips of Miss Fanny Elssler,[1] gives rise to a comment by M. Tastu, interesting in two respects: it provides a very reasonable explanation for one of St. Vincent Ferrier's miracles and also bears out an important fact in linguistic history. Here is the note:

> Though St. Vincent Ferrier wrote his sermons in Latin, he pronounced them in the Limousine tongue. The power he possessed of making his congregations understand him, although he spoke to them in a foreign idiom, was looked on as miraculous. Yet nothing could be more natural if one casts back one's mind to the age when Master Vincent flourished. At that time, the Romance languages spoken in the three great regions of the north, the centre, and the south, were practically identical; the various peoples, especially the educated classes, understood one another very well. Master Vincent was a success in England, Scotland, Ireland, Paris, Brittany, Italy, Spain and the Balearic Islands; the reason being that the inhabitants of all these countries understood, even if they could not speak it, a Romance language which was the sister, parent or cousin of the Valencian language, Vincent Ferrier's mother tongue.
>
> Besides, was not this famous evangelist a contemporary of Chaucer, John Froissart, Christina de Pisan, Boccaccio, Ausias March, and many other European celebrities?
>
> The Balearic peoples speak Limousine, which M. Raynouard has included without investigation or discrimination in Provençal. Majorcan has undergone fewer changes than any other of these old Romance dialects, being centred

[1] 1810-1884. Viennese dancer and rival to Taglioni.

in its islands where it is kept clean from all foreign contamination. The Langue d'Oc, even in its now decadent condition as the pleasant dialect of Montpellier and the surrounding country, offers the closest analogy to Majorcan, old and new. This is because the kings of Aragon, with their courts, often stayed in the city of Montpellier. Pedro II, killed at Muret in 1213 while fighting against Simon de Montfort, had married Mary, daughter of a Count of Montpellier, and became the father by her of James I, surnamed the Conqueror, who was born in Montpellier and spent his early childhood there. One of the characteristics that distinguish Majorcan from the other Romance dialects spoken in the South of France, are the definitive articles in popular use; most of these, and this is interesting, occur also in certain districts of the Island of Sardinia. Besides the neuter definite article *lo*, the masculine *el*, and the feminine *la*, we find the following:

Masc. sing.	Fem. sing.	Masc. plural	Fem. plural
so	*sa*	*sos*	*sas*
es	*es*	*ets*	*ets*
en	*na*	—	*nas*[1]

We should remark, however, that these articles, although of ancient use, have never been employed in the legal documents dating from the Aragonese conquest of the Balearics, which means that, here, as in the Italic lands, two languages were simultaneously spoken: the uneducated tongue, *plebea*, of vernacular use (this undergoes little alteration); and the language of scholarship and literature, *aulica illustra*, which is purified or improved by the passage of time, the progress of civilization, or the works of genius. Thus, at the present day, Castilian is the official written language of every Spanish province; yet each province has

[1] The *so*, *sos*, *sas* forms are now confined to Pollensa and Alcudia, where there is also a feminine form *u*, as in *U Seu*, the Cathedral. *En*, *na*, *nas* are used only as titles of honour in introducing proper names, as: *El rey en Jaume*, 'My lord King James'. Or humorously: *En Gelad*, 'My noble mule Frosty'.

kept its peculiar dialect for everyday use. In Majorca, Castilian is used only on formal occasions; normally you will hear nothing but Majorcan spoken, by either the nobility or the commons.[1] As you pass under a balcony where a young girl, an *Atlote* (from the Arabic *aila, lella*) is watering her flowers, it is in her soft native dialect that you hear her singing:

> *Sas atlotes, tots es diumenges,*
> *Quant no tenen res mes que fer,*
> *Van a regá es claveller,*
> *Dient-li: 'Beu jà que no menjes!'*

> The young girls every Sunday,
> When they have nothing better to do,
> Go watering the carnation pot,
> And tell it: 'Drink, since you do not eat!'

The music to which these words are set is in a key whose mournful Moorish cadences fill your heart and set you dreaming. But the girl's thrifty mother has heard her, and is quick to reply:

> *'Atlotes, filau! filau!*
> *Que sa camya se riu;*
> *Y sino l'apadassau,*
> *No v's arribor 'à estiu!'*

> 'Spin, girls, spin!
> For your shift is splitting (literally: 'the shift is smiling')
> And you will have to patch it
> If you want it to last the summer!'

Majorcan, especially when spoken by women, has for foreigners a gentle, graceful charm all its own. Here, when a woman bids good-bye in the following words: *'Bona nit*

[1] It is still the domestic language of all Majorcans from Cavaller to hired labourer, except for certain rich businessmen who want their children to be mistaken for Madrileños; but letters between Majorcans and their relations abroad are invariably written in Castilian, because none of them have learned to spell Majorcan. All newspapers must be printed in Castilian.

tenga! Es meu co no basta per di li: Adios!' 'Good night! I have not the heart to say: Good-bye!' it seems as if the soft cantilena could be recorded as a musical phrase.

After these specimens of the Majorcan vernacular, I shall allow myself to quote an example of the old courtly language. The *Mercader Mallorqui* ('The Majorcan Merchant'), a fourteenth-century troubadour, sings of the cruelties of his lady and takes leave of her thus:

Çercats d'uy may, jà siats bella e pros,
Equels vostres pres, e laus, e ris plesents,
Car vengut es lo temps que m'aurets mens.
No m'aucirá vostre 'sguard amoros,
Ne la semblança gaya;
Car trobat n'ay
Altra qui m'play
Sol que lui playa!
Altra, sens vos, per que l'in volray bé,
E tindr' en, car s'amor, que 'xi s' convé.

Henceforth, although lovely and high-born, you may search
For such deserts, such praises, such charming smiles as were yours alone,
For the time is come when you shall have me seldom at your side,
You shall no longer slay me with your amorous look,
And your pretended gaiety;
For I have found
Another who pleases me,
Might I but please her!

Like all Southern peoples, the Majorcans are born musicians and poets or, as their ancestors called them, 'troubadours', *trobadors*, which we might translate by 'improvisers'. The island of Majorca still contains several such, who enjoy a well-deserved reputation, among others two natives of Sóller. Fortunate, or unfortunate lovers, make a practice of visiting these troubadours who, for a consideration, and in accordance with the information supplied them, stand beneath girls' balconies, at a late hour of night, and sing improvised *coplas* of praise, complaint, sometimes even abuse, which they had been paid to compose. Foreigners, too, may treat themselves to this pleasure; in this island, it is not regarded as a matter of any consequence.[1]

[1] Serenading is now generally confined to the Eve of St. Ursula and the Eleven Thousand Virgins, whose feast falls on October 21st.

Chapter Fifteen

BEFORE continuing my narrative I must dwell upon the fanatical piety of the Valldemosan villagers with whom we had dealings, and describe the saint who is their great pride and whose simple cottage they showed us.

Valldemosa is the home of Catalina Tomás, who was beatified in 1792 by Pope Pius VI.[1] Several lives have been written of this holy virgin, her most recent biography being by Cardinal Antonio Despuig. The story has some charmingly ingenuous features. God, so the legend runs, having blessed His handmaid with discretion beyond her years, Catalina was seen to keep a strict fast on all the appointed days, long before reaching the age at which the Church ordains such observance.[2] From her earliest infancy she refrained from eating more than one meal a day. So ardent was her devotion to the Passion of the Redeemer, and the Sorrows of His Blessed Mother, that she always recited her rosary on country walks, using the leaves of olives or lentisk to tell the tens. Catalina's joy in seclusion and in religious exercises, together with a dislike of dances and other secular amusements, soon won her the name of *viejecita*, or 'little old woman'.[3] But her retirement and abstinence were rewarded by visits from the angels and all the company of Heaven: Jesus Christ, His Mother and the Saints came to serve her, the Virgin nursed her in sickness, St. Bruno raised her

[1] Canonized by Pope Pius X in 1935. Her image may be recognized by the white cake of fig-bread she carries.

[2] Catalina also covertly mixed sand with her soup to counteract the sin of gluttony. Although poor, she came of good family, an uncle owning the big estate of Son Geard—hence her popular title, 'The Lily of Son Gallart'.

[3] George Sand has misheard: she was called *Beateta*, 'The Little Saint', not *Veyata*, the Majorcan for *viejecita*.

when she fell, St. Anthony escorted her through the darkness of the night, carrying her pitcher and filling it at the well, St. Catherine dressed her namesake's hair and attended to her needs like a vigilant mother, St. Cosmo and St. Damian healed the wounds that she received in the course of her struggles with the Devil,[1] for Catalina's victory was not won without a fight; and finally St. Peter and St. Paul stood perpetually on either side to assist and defend her in temptation.

She accepted the Augustinian Rule in the convent of St. Magdalen at Palma,[2] where she set an example to her sisters in this Penitential Order, showing herself, as the Church tunefully prays, obedient, poor, chaste and lowly. Catalina's biographers ascribe to her the spirit of prophecy and the gift of miracles. One day, it is said, at a time when public prayers were offered in Majorca for the health of Pope Pius V, Catalina interrupted them suddenly, announcing that they were no longer needed because the Pontiff had departed from this world at that very hour, which proved to be true.

She died on April 5th, 1574, with the Psalmist's words on her lips: 'Lord, into Thy hands I commend my spirit!' Her death was regarded as a public disaster, and she was paid the highest honours. A devout Majorcan lady, Doña Juana de Pochs, replaced the wooden coffin, in which the holy virgin had originally been laid, by a splendid alabaster sepulchre ordered from Genoa; she also made a bequest for masses to be said both on the anniversary of the Blessed Catalina's translation and on the day of her patron, St. Catherine; and directed that a lamp be kept perpetually burning on her tomb. The body of the blessed virgin is preserved today in the Convent of Santa Eulalia,[3] where

[1] The Devil often rose to tempt her from the hole of the sink while she was washing up. I have the authentic sink in my house; it was taken from the cottage at Deyá (pulled down in 1931) where she lived for a while with an aunt.

[2] Fixed in the masonry at the back of the church of San Nicholás at Palma is the stone on which she had been sitting when the Virgin appeared and assured her that she would be admitted to the convent.

[3] Catalina's body, which rests in the church dedicated to her, not in the Convent of Santa Eulalia, is still occasionally displayed to the faithful. Its failure to decompose was taken as one more proof of holiness. Majorcan doctors hold that her ascetic diet of beans and vegetables facilitated this miracle.

Cardinal Despuig consecrated an altar and a religious service to her.

I have gladly related this little legend without omitting a word, in acknowledgement that there is such a thing as holiness, namely the true holiness possessed by ardent spirits. Although the visions and the zeal of the little girl from the Valldemosan hills no longer have the same religious meaning and philosophical import as the inspirations and ecstasies of Saints belonging to the Golden Age of Christianity, the *Viejecita Tomása* is none the less cousin-german to those other shepherdesses, the romantic St. Winifred and the sublime St. Joan of Arc. The Roman Church has never withheld places of honour in the Heavenly Kingdom from the humblest children of the people, though she now condemns and spurns those of her apostles who try to improve their earthly existence. Catalina the peasant girl was obedient, poor, chaste and lowly; but the Valldemosan peasants have benefited so little from her example, and so little understood her life, that one day when my son was sketching the ruins of the Charterhouse, they tried to stone him and his sister for what they regarded as desecration. They behaved exactly like the Church; as it were kindling the auto-da-fé pyre with one hand, and with the other burning incense before the effigies of her greater and lesser saints.

The village of Valldemosa has proudly claimed the status of a town since Moorish days—they called it Villa-Avente, a Roman name which, I imagine, had been given it by the Pisans or the Genoese [M. Tastu].[1] It lies in the lap of the mountain, level with the Charterhouse, of which it appears to be an annexe. The houses, like a cluster of sea-swallows' nests, are perched in an almost inaccessible spot, and the inhabitants, mostly fishermen, leave their homes at dawn and do not return until night.

[1] A force of Pisans and Genoese had briefly reconquered Majorca from the Moors in the eleventh century, but then sold it back to them. The name Vall de Mosa ('Valley of Moses') was perhaps due to a monkish fancy. On the slope facing the Charterhouse, near the top, stands a tall limestone rock easily mistakable for a hero's statue. Not far below its feet lies a pile of rocks, which look as though he had thrown them there. To the Carthusians this may have suggested Moses descending from Sinai in anger, after breaking the tables of the Law.

All day long the village is filled with the most talkative women in the world. Each sits on her doorstep busy cobbling her husband's breeches, a task that resembles his net-mending, and sings at the top of her voice. They are no less religious than the men; but with them religion is less intolerant, because more sincere. In this, at Valldemosa as everywhere else, the female sex is the superior. As a rule, women devote themselves to religious observances from enthusiasm, habit or conviction, whereas with men it is nine times out of ten a matter either of ambition or advantage. This was proved clearly enough under Louis XVIII and Charles X, when all major and minor posts in the government or in the army could be bought at the price of a confession-ticket or a mass.

The Majorcans' attachment to the monks is based upon greed, and I can best make this understood by quoting M. Marliani, whose views are all the more reliable because, on the whole, this historian of modern Spain shows himself hostile to the action taken in 1836, when the monasteries were suddenly dissolved.

'Being considerate landowners,' he writes, 'and paying small attention to their wealth, the monks had built up a community of interests between the peasants and themselves; tenant-farmers cultivating the monastery lands suffered little hardship, either in the amount of rent, or in its regular collection. The monks, having no posterity to consider, did not hoard their gains and, as soon as their estates produced enough to meet the material needs of the community, were very easy-going with regard to the remainder. Thus a sudden despoliation of the monks upset the peasants' economy: they understood only too well that the Government and the new landlords would ask more of them than had a guild of parasites without family or social ties. The beggars who swarmed about the refectory doors were no longer given the broken meats from the monastery tables.'

Carlism among the Majorcan peasants can be accounted for on material grounds only, since one could certainly not find a province less bound to Spain by patriotic feeling, or a people less inclined to excite themselves over politics. The secret prayers they offered for the restoration of the ancient régime proved that they were terrified of any new upheaval, whatever it might be; and the alarm which, at the time of our stay, caused the island to be placed in a state of siege, startled the adherents of Don Carlos in Majorca hardly less than the supporters of Queen Isabella. This alarm was characteristic, I shall not say of the Majorcans' timidity (doubtless they would make very good soldiers),[1] but of the concern for their property and a desire to see their peace undisturbed.

An old priest dreamed one night that robbers had broken into his house. He sprang out of bed in a great fright, still under the influence of this nightmare, and woke his housekeeper. She, catching his terror, although ignorant of what had caused it, roused the whole neighbourhood with her screams. The scare spread throughout the hamlet, and thence throughout the island. All ears buzzed with the news that a Carlist army had landed, and the Captain-General heard the evidence of the priest who, whether ashamed to take back what he had said, or not yet recovered from his nightmare, asserted that he had seen the enemy. Measures were at once taken to meet the danger: a state of siege was declared at Palma, and every soldier in the island recalled to the Colours. But nothing came into view, not a bush stirred and no foreign footprint (as in Robinson Crusoe's isle) was imprinted on the sandy shores. The authorities punished the wretched priest for having made them look foolish: instead of sending him about his business as a dreamer, they confined him in prison as a fomenter of sedition. Yet the precautionary measures were not revoked and, when we left Majorca, at the time of the Maroto executions, the state of siege remained in force.

How odd was the reticence which the Majorcans seemed impelled to observe in face of such events as then convulsed Spain! No one mentioned them, unless in a whisper to his own family circle. We thought it incredible that such suspicious mistrust could prevail in a country so free of vindictiveness or oppression. The Palma newspaper articles were the most ludicrous documents I have ever read, and I much regret that I did not bring away a few numbers as specimens of Majorcan polemics.

[1] In defence of their island at least.

But the following is, without exaggeration, the sort of comment made on the significance and authenticity of the news items then coming to hand:

> However well-established these events may appear in the eyes of persons inclined to welcome them, we cannot too strongly advise that our readers await the sequel before passing any judgement. The thoughts which spring to mind in the face of such occurrences call for mature consideration, and at the same time a certainty which, though we do not wish to cloud it with doubt, neither will we rashly undertake to anticipate. The fate of Spain is shrouded in a veil that will now soon be raised, but on which no one must lay an ill-advised hand before the decisive hour. Until then we shall refrain from giving our opinion, and shall advise all wise minds to withhold their verdict on the actions of the various parties, until they see the situation assume clearer outlines.

Caution and reserve are the ruling trends of the Majorcan character, as they themselves are the first to admit. A peasant will always acknowledge a countryside greeting, but if a single additional word is addressed to him, even in his own dialect, by someone whom he does not know, he will be most chary of replying. A foreign appearance is enough to scare him, and he will go far out of his way to avoid an encounter.

We could have lived on good terms with these worthy folk, had we only put in an appearance at Church. This would not have prevented them from holding us to ransom on every conceivable excuse; but we should at least have been able to walk across their fields without the risk of being hit on the head by a stone as we passed a thicket. This precautionary measure, however, did not at once occur to us, and almost to the end of our stay we remained unaware how profoundly our way of life shocked them. They called us heathen, Mohammedans—or Jews, which they think the worst of all. The mayor drew his underlings' attention to us as legitimate objects of disapproval; and for all I know the priest may have preached against us. My daughter's loose jacket and trousers also offended local sentiment deeply. It was thought disgraceful that a 'young person', nine years of age, should scour the mountains 'disguised as a man'. Nor were the peasants alone in this affectation of prudishness.[1]

The post-horn, which on Sundays echoed through the village and along the roads, summoning laggards to mass, met with no response from us in the Charterhouse. At first we were deaf through a failure to understand the summons, but when we did understand it, we became deafer still. The villagers then proceeded to avenge the glory of God in a most un-Christian manner: banding together in a refusal to sell us their fish, eggs or vegetables except at prohibitive cost. We were not allowed to quote market prices or normal values. At the slightest objection a peasant would reply with the air of a Spanish grandee: 'You don't want any? Then you shan't have any!' and replacing the onions or potatoes in his sack, would stalk augustly away and could not be recalled to reach an agreement. The punishment thus inflicted on us for bargaining was to go hungry; and it proved effective because these peasants would not undersell one another. Indeed, the next man who came to our door asked twice as much as the first, and the third three times as much; so that we were at their mercy and forced to live like hermits, paying more than would have kept us in princely style at Paris. Our only way out of this difficulty was to persuade the French Consul's cook to send us supplies from Palma. He was our good angel, and had I been a Roman Emperor, I should have set his night-cap among the constellations. But on wet days no carrier was willing to venture out at any price; and since it rained on and off for two months, we frequently nibbled bread as hard as ship's biscuit and dined like true Carthusians.

Had we all been in good health, this would have been a minor trial. I am naturally abstemious and even stoical in my diet. My children's magnificent appetites made a silk purse out of every sow's ear and a dish for a king out of a green lemon.

[1] In the last two years, finding modern skirts not warm enough, the olive-pickers of Valldemosa have taken to trousers—though wearing smocks over them for decency's sake.

The boy, who had been weak and sickly when I brought him from France, took on a new lease on life, and cured a dangerous rheumatic complaint by scampering from dawn to dusk, like a liberated hare, among the tall mountain plants, soaked to the waist. Mother Nature and the grace of Providence together worked this miracle for him; he was by no means a strong child.

Our other invalid, however, far from thriving on the hardships and the damp, had fallen into an alarming decline. Although the entire medical faculty of Palma pronounced him a hopeless case, he had no chronic complaint whatsoever; but he had caught cold, and the after-effects, emphasized by the lack of a strengthening diet, plunged him into a listless condition from which he could not emerge. He resigned himself to this, as one can do if the suffering is one's own; but we could not resign ourselves to seeing him suffer, and for the first time in my life I became seriously distressed by trifling annoyances. I would fly into a passion when the soup was too peppery or had been dipped into by the servant, and tear my hair because a fresh loaf had either not arrived or had been turned into a sponge while the mule forded the torrent. I have absolutely no recollection of what I ate in Pisa or Trieste; but if I live to be a hundred, I shall never forget the arrival of the provision basket at the Charterhouse. I would have given anything in the world for a daily cup of nourishing beef-tea and a glass of Bordeaux to offer our invalid! Majorcan food and the way it was prepared when we did not supervise and assist in the cooking, aroused an insuperable disgust in him. His feelings proved well-justified when one day a skinny chicken was served at table and we saw hopping on its smoking back a number of huge *Herrenflöhe*, which Hoffmann might have presented as evil spirits, but which he would certainly not have accepted as a garnish. My children were overcome by such hearty laughter at the sight that they nearly fell under the table.[1]

The invariable basis of all Majorcan cooking is the pig, in every conceivable form and manner of presentation. It might well have been Majorca which the Little Chimney-sweep described in the story, when he praised his inn and said admiringly

[1] I suspect an elaborate joke by the children to disgust their elders.

that five kinds of meat were eaten there: swine's flesh, crackling, bacon, ham and salt pork. I am sure that more than two thousand different dishes are prepared from the pig in Majorca, and at least two hundred kinds of black pudding, so liberally seasoned with garlic, black and red pepper and corrosive spices of every sort, that you hazard your life with every bite. Twenty dishes may appear on the table, all looking like every kind of Christian food: but beware, they are hellish brews cooked by the Devil himself. Finally, for dessert, comes a handsome open pastry dusted with something that looks innocuously like sugar, and decorated with slices of fruit suggesting oranges. This turns out to be a garlic-flavoured pork-tart; the fruit are *tomatigas* (tomatoes) and sweet peppers; and the sugar, table salt. Chickens, though numerous, are nothing but skin and bone. At Valldemosa we should doubtless have been taxed a *reál* on every grain of corn we bought to fatten them. The sea-fish sold to us was as tasteless and dry as the chickens.

One day we bought a large *calamar*, or cuttlefish, for the sake of examining it. I have never seen a more repulsive creature. Its body was as large as a turkey-cock's, its eyes as big as oranges, and its limp, hideous tentacles, when uncurled, were four or five feet long. The fishermen assured us that it was a great delicacy. We were not tempted by its appearance, but paid homage to Maria Antonia for the way she prepared and sampled it with a great smacking of lips.[1]

If these worthy folk smiled at our excitement over the cuttlefish, our turn came a few days later. As we came down the mountain we saw peasants leaving their tasks and rushing towards some travellers who had halted in the road and were carrying a basket containing a pair of wonderful, rare, amazing, incomprehensible birds. The entire population of the mountain was set agog by the appearance of this species of unknown feathered fowl. 'What do they eat?' they wondered aloud, as they stared. 'Perhaps they don't eat at all!' someone answered. . . .

[1] In the winter months, the Valldemosa fishermen rarely catch any fish but cackerel (a dull sort of sprat) and *calamar*, which is indeed a delicacy, especially when softened in a pressure-cooker. Veteran *calamars* are occasionally caught with tentacles between one foot and eighteen inches long.

'Do they live on land or on sea?' 'They probably spend the whole time in the air.' The two birds had nearly been suffocated by the general admiration, before we discovered that they were neither condors, phœnixes, nor hippogryphs, but fine farmyard geese, which a wealthy squire was sending as a gift to a country neighbour.

In Majorca, as in Venice, liqueur-like wines are plentiful and of the finest quality. The muscatel wine which we usually drank was as good and as inexpensive as the Cyprian wine of the Adriatic coast. But the local red wines, the proper preparation of which is an art unknown to the Majorcans, were harsh, dark, burning, of high alcoholic content and more expensive than our plainest French table wines. These hot, heady wines were so bad for our invalid, and for us too, that we nearly always drank the water, which was excellent.[1] It may have been the purity of this spring water that produced a certain rapid and noticeable change in us: our teeth had taken on a whiteness that no cosmetic art could have given the most elegant Parisian. But the reason may equally well have lain in our enforced abstemiousness. Since we had no butter and could not stomach the grease, the nauseating oil, and the incendiary methods of the native kitchen, we lived on lean meat, fish and vegetables, all seasoned, by way of sauce, with water from the torrent; and as an occasional indulgence flavoured this with the juice of a sour orange freshly picked from our garden.[2] On the other hand, our desserts were magnificent: candied sweet potatoes from Malaga, candied peel from Valencia, and grapes worthy of the land of Canaan. These grapes, white or red, are of oblong shape, and rather thick-skinned, which helps to preserve them throughout the winter. They are exquisite, and you can eat as many of them as you like without suffering from the flatulence produced by ours. Fontainebleau grapes are juicier and fresher; but those of Majorca sweeter and of firmer flesh. The latter are a food, the former a drink. A painter's admiration would have been roused

[1] They should have tried tempering the wine with water in Majorcan, or Classical Greek, style. The alcoholic content varies from twelve to fourteen per cent.

[2] In Majorca oranges ripen in January.

by the clusters on the monastery vines, some of which weighed between twenty and twenty-five pounds.[1] These were what sustained us in times of food shortage. The peasants thought that they had done very well by charging us four times their value; little knowing that this was still nothing compared with the price of French grapes, so that both parties to the sale had the pleasure of laughing up their sleeves. We never had occasion to haggle over cactus-figs: which are by far the most horrible fruit I ever tasted.[2]

If these frugal living-conditions had not, as I have already said, produced a bad, even a fatal, effect on one of us, the others would have found them tolerable enough. Even in a deserted Majorcan Charterhouse, and at daggers drawn with the wiliest peasants in the world, we had managed to surround ourselves with some degree of comfort. We possessed window-panes, doors, and a stove, a unique stove which the best blacksmith in Palma had taken a month to forge, and which cost us a hundred francs. It was a simple iron cylinder with a pipe leading out through the window, but took at least an hour to light, and then quickly turned red-hot; so that after having kept the doors open all this time, to clear the room of smoke, we opened them again almost at once to cool it. Besides, the so-called stove-expert had lined the inside, by way of cement, with a certain by-product of the cow which, for religious reasons, Indians plaster on the walls of their houses and even on their persons, the cow being notoriously regarded among them as a sacred animal. Whatever cathartic effect the holy odour arising from the burning of this substance may have on the soul, I can testify that it is far from a delight to the senses. This cement did not dry for a month, and meanwhile we could easily imagine ourselves in the particular circle of the Inferno where Dante claims that he saw the sycophants. Vainly I asked myself what crime of this nature could have condemned me to such torment, what Power I had fawned on, which Pope or King my flatteries had

[1] Such huge clusters have never been seen since; and why were they left hanging on the vines until mid-December?

[2] Greatly esteemed by Majorcans; but most foreigners find them insipid, and are not clever in removing the thin, cruel spines which cover the scarlet rind.

encouraged in his grandiose follies. I could not find so much as an office-boy or porter on my conscience; and when did I ever bow to a policeman or a journalist? Luckily, the Carthusian apothecary could sell us some exquisite gum-benzoin, left over from the supply of perfumes recently burned as incense before God's image in his monastery church; and this heavenly emanation fought and conquered the fumes of the Inferno's eighth trench.

Our furniture was magnificent: trestle-beds with which nobody could have quarrelled; clean, new mattresses, though not very soft and more expensive than in Paris; and those fine large coverlets, made of quilted and padded chintz, purchasable for a fair enough price from the Palma Jews. A French lady who lived in Majorca[1] kindly lent us several pounds of feathers, which she had ordered for her own use from Marseilles, and with these we made our invalid a couple of pillows. This was indeed the height of luxury in a country where geese are regarded as beings from another world, and chickens still itch when they descend from the spit.

We had several tables, numerous straw-bottomed chairs like those seen in French peasants' cottages; also a voluptuous deal sofa, and cushions for it of wool-stuffed ticking. The uneven and crumbling floor of the cell was covered with those long-strawed Valencian mats which resemble sun-yellowed turf, and with those splendid long-haired sheepskins, of admirable quality and whiteness, which the Majorcans know how to dress very well.

As in Africa and the East, there are few cupboards in the old houses of Majorca, and none at all in the Carthusians' cells. Since one is expected to lock up one's possessions in big deal

[1] Doña Elena Choussat de Canut, the eventual owner of the Pleyel piano. She records that when George Sand arrived in Palma, the women avoided her like the plague, outraged by her reputation. According to her account, George wore black or dark clothes in Palma, around her neck a black velvet ribbon supporting a large diamond cross, and on her wrist a bracelet enriched with certain jewelled mementoes. She had beautiful plaits of hair, caught with a silver dagger; and when she once went to the theatre with M. Fleury, the French Consul, all opera glasses were fixed on her. Although smoking at home, or when out on walks, she never did so in other people's houses.

chests, our yellow leather trunks could pass for elegant pieces of furniture. A big, multi-coloured tartan shawl, used as a foot-rug on our journey, now became a magnificent curtain to screen the alcove, and my son enlivened the stove with one of those delightful clay vases from the town of Felanitx, shaped and decorated in pure Moorish style.

Felanitx ought to supply Europe with these exquisitely shaped little water-coolers. They are so light that one would think them made of cork, and of so fine a texture as to seem like some precious material. The porous clay lets the water seep through, so that the vase empties in less than six hours. I am no physicist, and my observations may seem ingenuous; but I often thought our vase was under a wonderful spell. We used to leave it filled to the brim on top of the red-hot stove-plate, and sometimes, when all the water had escaped, the vase itself stayed dry and unbroken; yet while a single drop of water remained, this was always icy cold, even though the wood we laid to dry beside it were scorched by the heat. Our lovely vase, crowned with a wreath of ivy dragged from the wall outside, pleased the artistic eye more than all your modern gilt Sèvres porcelain.

The Pleyel piano, wrested from the hands of the customs officials after three weeks of negotiations and four hundred francs paid in dues, filled the lofty, echoing vault of the cell with a glorious sound.[1] Finally, the sacristan had been persuaded to move into our cell a large splendid Gothic chair of carved oak, which was being eaten away by worm and rats in a disused Carthusian chapel. Its frame served us as a book-case, while after dark, by the gleam of lamplight, its pierced fretwork and tapering spires cast on the wall a rich, lacy shadow with magnificent pinnacles, and completely restored the ancient monastic character of the cell.

Our ex-landlord, Señor Gomez, the wealthy individual who

[1] Chopin left this piano behind because the export rights would have cost too much. Nobody, however, would buy it, for fear that the infection might carry off the next person to play on it. Only Doña Elena Choussat de Canut, the Frenchwoman who had given the feathers for Chopin's pillow, was unafraid. She sold her own piano to a neighbour, paid Chopin the money, and kept the Pleyel for herself. It is now shown in the Valldemosa cell, together with other Chopin and Sand relics.

had let Son Vent to us, but secretly, since it is not respectable for a Majorcan to speculate with his property, made a great scene and threatened legal action because we had damaged a few earthenware plates, for which he made us pay as though they had been porcelain. He also bullied us into paying for the whitewashing and redecoration of the entire house, to disinfect it after our invalid's catarrh. However, it is an ill wind that blows nobody any good, since in his anxiety to be rid of everything we had touched, he was eager to sell us all the Son Vent household linen. We were therefore not forced to sow flax in the hope of getting sheets and table-cloths at some distant date, like the Italian nobleman who promised shirts to his pages; but he did insist on charging for his old linen at the price of new.

My readers must not accuse me of childishness when I describe annoyances which assuredly have left me with no deeper resentment than the hole in my purse; for no one will deny that the most interesting subject of study in any foreign country is certainly the people. When I say, moreover, that among the Majorcans I met with shameless dishonesty and gross greed in every single monetary dealing, however trifling; and when I add that while pretending to be shocked by our lack of faith, they flaunted their own religious devotion, my readers will agree that the piety of simple souls, now so highly extolled by certain Conservatives, is not always the most edifying and ethical phenomenon. And that we should be allowed, if we so wish, to desire a different way of understanding and worshipping God Yes, I have heard the same commonplaces recited over and over again: that it is criminal and dangerous to undermine even a misguided and corrupt faith when one has nothing to put in its place; that the only moral, hospitable, and sincere peoples are those uncontaminated by the poison of philosophical inquiry and revolutionary hysteria; that poetry, greatness, and the ancient virtues still flourish among them, etc., etc. . . And, I admit, these solemn arguments sounded rather funnier in Majorca than elsewhere. When I saw my children, brought up in that abomination of desolation, Philosophy, gladly helping and attending to a sick friend, shouldering the task entirely alone, while one hundred and sixty thousand Majorcans would have turned away, with the most cruel lack of feeling and the most abject terror, from an illness supposed to be infectious, I told myself that there was more right-thinking and charity in my little scoundrels than in that whole population of saints and apostles.[1]

Those devout servants of God did not fail, however, to accuse me of a great crime in exposing my children to the infection, and prophesied that Heaven, to punish my blindness, would visit them both with the same disease. I replied that, in our family, if one of us had the plague, the others would stay beside him; and that in France it was no more the custom to desert the sick, since the Revolution, than it had been before; that at the time of the Napoleonic Wars, Spanish prisoners suffering from the most deadly diseases had wandered through our countryside, and the peasants, after providing bowls of soup and linen, had made over their beds to them and acted as sick-nurses; that several peasants had fallen victims to such charity and died of the infection, but that this did not prevent the survivors from continuing to exercise charitable hospitality. The Majorcans shook their heads with pitying smiles.[2] They found the idea of selfless service to a stranger as incomprehensible as that of behaving honestly or even obligingly to a foreigner.

Travellers who have visited the interior of the island wonder at the disinterested hospitality of the Majorcan farmer. They write admiringly that despite the absence of inns it is none the less easy and pleasant to tour the country, where a simple letter of introduction will cause one to be welcomed and entertained with open arms, free of charge. As I see it, that letter of introduction is not quite so simple a document as might appear. These travellers omit to mention that all classes in Majorca, and hence all the inhabitants, are linked by a community of interests which establishes friendly relations among themselves, but in which neither religious charity nor human feeling plays any part.

[1] A family in the neighbouring parish of Deyá bears the nickname *Catolica* because their ancestors elected to stay behind in the village and nurse plague victims, when the order had been given to evacuate it.

[2] Not understanding French.

A few words will suffice to explain the pecuniary circumstances.

Although rich in capital, the aristocracy are poor in income, and ruined by the loans that they have been obliged to raise. The Jews,[1] who are numerous and rich in ready money, hold all the Cavallers' lands in their wallets, and are the real owners of the island; thus the Cavallers are no more than aristocratic representatives commissioned to do the honours of their domains and palaces, one for the other, as well as for the occasional foreigners who visit the island. To fulfil these exalted functions in proper style, they must annually borrow from the Jews, and every year the snowball grows bigger. In the first part of this book I explained that Majorcan economic life is paralysed by a lack of openings for industry; but the indigent Cavallers make it a point of honour to achieve ruin in their own good time, peacefully and quietly, without abandoning the luxury, or rather the spendthrift liberality, of their ancestors. The interests of the speculators are therefore closely linked with those of the farmers, a part of whose rents they collect by virtue of the title-deeds made over to them by the Cavallers.

Thus the peasant, who perhaps profits by this division of his debts, pays as little as possible to his lord, and as much as possible to the banker. The lord is resigned to his position of helpless dependence, the Jew is relentless but patient. He makes concessions, feigns great tolerance, allows time to pay, but pursues his end with devilish genius: once he has his clutches on an estate, sooner or later it must all come to him; and his interest is to prove indispensable until the debt reaches the value of the security. In twenty years' time no landed aristocracy will be left in Majorca.[2] The Jews will establish themselves in power, as they have done in France, and raise their heads which are now still bowed in feigned humility beneath the ill-disguised scorn of the nobility and the childish hatred of the common people. Meanwhile the peasant quakes before them. He turns sadly to his old master and, weeping affectionate tears, extracts

[1] It is not clear which Jews are intended. Perhaps she means the Catholic *Xuetas*, many of whom were money-lenders.

[2] After nearly one hundred and twenty years, the Cavallers still own great estates; incidentally, some of them are descended from the Jewish converts of 1453.

the largest share he can from the remnants of the ancient fortune. His interest lies in satisfying both these powers, and obliging them as far as possible, lest he be crushed between them. Provide yourself, therefore, with an introduction to one of the peasants, whether from a nobleman or from a rich businessman makes no odds—who else would give such a thing, since there is no middle class in Majorca?—and the peasant's door will at once open to you. But try asking for a glass of water without an introduction, and watch what happens!

Yet the Majorcan peasant is a gentle, kind creature, with peaceful habits and a tranquil, patient nature. He has no love of evil, and no knowledge of good. He goes to confession, prays, and thinks incessantly of how to earn an entry to Paradise, yet is ignorant of the true obligations of human kind. You can no more hate him than you could an ox or a sheep, for he is close to the savage, whose soul is lulled in animal innocence. He recites his prayers like the superstitious savage; but he would eat his fellow-man without a qualm, were that the custom of his country, and were he unable to satisfy himself fully with pork. He cheats, extorts, lies, abuses and plunders without the least scruple, where foreigners are concerned, not regarding these as fellow-men. Though he would never rob his neighbour of so much as an olive, he believes that in God's scheme of things the only use for human beings from overseas is to bring the Majorcans nice little profits.

We nicknamed Majorca 'Monkey Island' because, when surrounded by these crafty, thieving and yet innocent creatures, we grew accustomed to defending ourselves against them, but felt no more resentment or scorn than Indians feel towards chimpanzees[1] or mischievous, timid orang-utangs.

Although you may grow hardened to the sight of these people wearing human shape and stamped with the seal of God, who lead so aimless an existence in a region isolated from contemporary humanity, it is sad nevertheless that these imperfect beings are gifted with powers of understanding and perfectibility, that they share a common destiny with more advanced

[1] Indians seldom meet chimpanzees, which are natives of West Africa; and have to visit the East Indies for a view of the orang-utang.

races, and that it is only a matter of time—an interval seemingly long to us, but negligible in the abyss of eternity—before they achieve it. Though this interval does not appear to trouble Providence, it frightens and distresses you as an ephemeral being; the greater your awareness of their potential goodness, the more you suffer to see them fettered by chains of the past. You feel in your heart, your mind, the depths of your soul, that every other human life is bound up with your own, that nobody can live without loving or being loved, understanding or being understood, helping or being helped. Only the proud derive pleasure from a sense of intellectual and moral superiority. I imagine that the fond desire of all generous people is not that they should themselves sink to the level of their inferiors, but that they should raise to their own, in the twinkling of an eye, everything lying beneath them, and thus live at last the true life of sympathy, intercourse, equality and brotherhood, which is the religious ideal of the human conscience.

I am certain that this desire lurks at the bottom of every heart, and that in those of us who struggle against it, and think that they have choked it with specious arguments, a strange, bitter nameless pain arises. The lower classes wear themselves out or wither away because they cannot rise and, of the higher classes, some grow angry and impatient from vainly stretching out a helping hand, while those who make no such gesture become consumed by boredom and the terrors of solitude, until they sink into an existence more bestial than that enjoyed by the lowest of the low.

Chapter Sixteen

So we were alone in Majorca, no less isolated than if we had been living in a desert; and when we had done battle with the monkeys and won our daily bread, we used to sit together around the stove and laugh at it all. But as the winter continued, every attempt at cheerfulness and calm was frozen in my breast by the gloom. Our invalid's health continued to deteriorate, the wind sobbed in the ravine, the rain beat on our window-panes, the voice of the thunder penetrated our thick walls and its gloomy note mingled with the children's laughter and games. The sea-eagles and bearded vultures,[1] emboldened by the mist, swooped down to devour our wretched sparrows on the very pomegranate-tree which blocked my window. Heavy seas prevented all boats from leaving the shelter of their coves; we felt ourselves prisoners far from enlightened help or effectual sympathy. We could almost see Death hovering over our heads, waiting to seize the sufferer, whom we were single-handedly battling to keep alive. No human being within reach but would willingly have hastened him towards the grave, so as to remove the alleged danger of his proximity. This thought became horribly depressing, though we felt strong enough in ourselves to make up to one another, by solicitude and affection, for the help and sympathy that were denied us. At such times of trial the heart normally expands, and affection is ennobled and reinvigorated by the great strength which it derives from a sense of human solidarity So it grieved us to find our lot cast among beings who neither thought nor felt as we did and who, far

[1] Bearded vultures still breed on the Gran Puig, but I have never heard of their raiding a village. Perhaps Maria Antonia offered the vultures as an excuse for the disappearance of chickens from the outside kitchen.

from showing any sympathy, became themselves the objects of our deepest pity.

I was also exercised and perplexed by my complete lack of scientific knowledge; aware that none but a truly great doctor could treat this sickness, the responsibility for which weighed like lead on my heart. The doctor who visited us, and whose skill and industry I do not question, made a false diagnosis, as any doctor may, even the most famous; every genuine practitioner admits that he has done so time and time again. Our invalid's bronchitis was now succeeded by a nervous condition which produced several symptoms of laryngeal phthisis. Though the doctor had observed these symptoms on certain occasions, he had taken no stock of contrary symptoms that were obvious to me in permanent attendance on his patient, and therefore prescribed a régime suitable for consumptives: namely bleeding, starvation and a milk diet. We all thought that this was a mistake. The invalid himself realized that bleeding would be fatal; and I, who had nursed many sick people, felt the same foreboding, despite my ignorance of medicine.[1] I was terrified, however, to rely on what might be a deceptive instinct and pit this against the assertions of a skilled physician; so that when I saw the disease gaining ground, I fell a prey to torments which everyone will understand. 'A bleeding might save him,' I was told. 'If you refuse to let him undergo it, he will die.' But an inner voice assured me even in my sleep: 'A bleeding must kill him, and if you save him from it, he will live.' I am convinced that this was the voice of Providence, and now that our friend, the terror of Majorca, is acknowledged to be no more consumptive than I am,[2] I thank Heaven for not having destroyed the faith which saved us.

Starvation did not suit him at all. When we saw its ill effects, we complied with it as little as possible; but alas, there was no middle course to follow between the scorching local spiced meats and the most meagre diet. Milk and milk products, the

[1] Yet she prided herself on being the pharmacist and physician of her Nohant villagers.

[2] This version of the book, written in 1839, is dated 1855; yet Chopin had succumbed to consumption in October 1849.

harmful effects of which we came to appreciate later, were fortunately scarce enough in Majorca not to do him any harm. At that time we still thought milk would work wonders, and took great pains to procure a supply. There are no cows on those mountains, and the goat's milk we bought had always been sampled on the way by the children who delivered it, though this did not prevent the jug from reaching us fuller than when it started. The miracle was performed every morning for whatever devout messenger remembered to say his prayers in the monastery courtyard—beside the well. To put an end to these religious phenomena, we purchased a goat. She was the most gentle and lovable creature in the world, a lovely little African nanny, not yet two years old, with short chamois-coloured hair, a smooth hornless head, a pronounced Roman nose and drooping ears. These goats differ greatly from ours. They have the same cervine coat and ovine profile, but not the arch, saucy countenance of our playful kids. On the contrary, they seem full of melancholy. They also differ from ours in having tiny udders that yield very little milk. When they are fully grown, this milk has a wild, tart flavour highly esteemed by the Majorcans, but most offensive to us.

Our pet was enjoying her first maternity, and her milk had a delicate taste; but she was like a miser, especially when, parted from the herd among which she had been accustomed—no, not to gambol, being too solemn, too Majorcan for that—to stand musing on the top of the mountain, she fell into a state of gloom which was in certain respects analogous to our own. Though many fine weeds flourished in our courtyard, and aromatic plants, once tended by the Carthusians, were still to be found in our small garden, nothing could reconcile her to captivity. She wandered bewildered and disconsolate through the cloisters, bleating so pitifully that it would have moved a heart of stone. To keep her company we bought a fat sheep, with a thick white fleece six inches long, one of a breed now seen in France only on toy-sellers' counters, or on our grandmothers' fans. This admirable companion somewhat restored the goat's tranquillity, and herself gave us a fairly creamy milk. But although well-fed, they produced so little between the two of them, that we soon suspected the frequent visits paid by Maria Antonia, the Niña, and Catalina to our livestock. We therefore put them under lock and key in a small yard at the foot of the church-tower, and did the milking ourselves. Their thin milk made a quite wholesome and pleasant infusion when mixed with milk of almonds, which my children and I took turns in expressing. There was hardly anything else we could use. All the drugs obtainable in Palma were insufferably dirty. The badly refined sugar imported there from Spain is dark and oily, with a strong purgative effect on those who are unaccustomed to it.

One day we saw some violets growing in a wealthy farmer's garden, and thought our troubles were at an end. He gave us permission to pick some for an infusion, and when we had gathered our little bunch, charged us for it at the rate of five centimes a violet: one Majorcan sou being the equivalent of three French ones.

In addition to these domestic cares, we had to sweep our rooms and make the beds ourselves if we wanted to sleep at night; because the Majorcan maid could not touch them without at once imparting to us, with insupportable bounty, the same creatures which my children had been so amused to discover on the back of that roast chicken. Very few hours were left for work and walks; but these we employed well. The children took pains over their lessons, and when they were done we had only to emerge from the cell to find ourselves in the most diverse and admirable landscape, framed by vast mountains. Some fortuitously picturesque scene presented itself at every step: a little chapel perched on a sheer rock, a crannied cliff, a hermitage set beside a spring full of tall reeds, a clump of trees planted among huge, ivy-mantled boulders. When the sun condescended to appear for a moment, all the plants, stones and rain-sodden wastes at once sparkled with incredibly brilliant colours.

Two of our walks proved to be of particular interest. The memory of the first is not pleasant to me, despite the perfect views, because our invalid, who was in good health at that time (it was during our stay at Son Vent)[1] wanted to come with us, and the resultant exhaustion induced his illness. Our goal was

[1] He was 'sick as a dog' at Son Vent. See p. 48.

a hermitage three miles from the Charterhouse. We followed the right arm of the mountain-range, climbing from hill to hill, up a stony path which cut our feet in pieces, until we reached the northern coast. At each turn of the path we saw the sea stretched out magnificently, far below us, and a belt of beautiful vegetation lying between us and it. I had never before seen fertile shores, clothed with trees and shrubs down to the first wave, instead of the usual white cliffs, dreary salt flats or muddy beaches.[1] In every part of the French coast that I know, even the heights of Port-Vendres, where at last I experienced its full beauty, I have always thought the sea dirty or disagreeable to approach. Even the famous Lido of Venice is a horribly bare stretch of sand, inhabited by huge lizards that dart out in thousands from under your feet and seem to be chasing you in ever increasing numbers, as in a nightmare. At Royant, at Marseilles, almost everywhere I believe, on our coasts, a belt of sticky seaweed and a desert of sand spoil our approach to the sea. In Majorca alone I finally saw the sea of my dreams, clear and blue as the sky, like a sapphire plain carefully ploughed into gently undulating furrows which,[2] if you are looking down from a certain height, seem quite still and framed by dark green forests. Every step on the winding mountain path offered us a new view, each more superb than the last. We had to climb down a long way before we reached the hermitage. Yet this part of the coast, although very lovely, did not have that majestic quality which I found at another point some months later.

The four or five hermits were most unromantic.[3] Their dwelling place is as wretched and crude as their profession implies: and below their terrace garden, which they were engaged in digging when we arrived, a great lonely expanse of sea stretched before their eyes. We discovered them to be the stupidest people in the world. They wore no religious habit. Their superior left his spade and came up to us in a shapeless jacket of brownish

[1] This was an optical illusion. The coast at this point is precipitous and iron-bound.

[2] There must have been a swell. On calm days the sea is glassy and marked as far as the horizon with broad wavy bands of paler blue, formed by currents.

[3] The hermits now sell pickled samphire, coloured ribbons and postcards to pilgrims; and have been allowed to resume their brown habits.

colour; his short hair and dirty beard were by no means picturesque. He spoke of the hard life he led, and of the unendurable cold prevailing on this coast; but when we asked him whether it ever froze, our concerted efforts failed to make him understand what frost is. He did not know the word in any language, and had never heard of any countries colder than the island of Majorca. However, he had some idea of France through having seen our fleet sail past in 1830, on its way to capture Algiers; this had been the finest, the most wonderful, one might say the only sight of his life. He asked us whether the French had succeeded in taking Algiers, and when we told him that they had recently also taken Constantine,[1] his eyes opened wide and he exclaimed that the French were a great nation.

Then he led us to an extremely dirty little cell, and introduced us to the senior hermit. We took him for a centenarian, but were amazed to learn that he was a mere forty-four years[2] of age. He looked a complete imbecile, despite his grimy, shaking hands that still went on automatically carving wooden spoons. Although not deaf, he paid us no attention until the superior addressed him, when he raised a huge head, like a wax-work, and showed us his hideously sottish countenance. A lifetime of intellectual degradation was etched in that wretched drawn face, and I hastily averted my eyes from one of the most terrifying and painful sights I had ever witnessed. We gave them alms, because they belong to a mendicant Order; still greatly respected by the peasants, who see that they lack for nothing. As I returned to Palma by way of the Charterhouse, a violent wind arose and blew us over several times, which made progress so tiring that our invalid was exhausted by the effort.

We took the second walk a few days before our departure from Majorca. Never has the sight of natural beauty made a greater impact on me or left so indelible an impression. Indeed, I doubt whether I have been equally affected by any experience more than three or four times in my life.

The rains had at last ceased, and spring suddenly began to

[1] Capital of the province by that name, lying between Algeria and Tunis.

[2] He was an octogenarian: the monk apparently raised four fingers twice to signify 'eighty', not 'forty-four'. See p. 198.

unfold. We were now in February, with all the almond-trees in bloom, and fragrant jonquils starring the meadows. Apart from the colour of the sky and the bright tints of the landscape, this was the one noticeable difference between spring and winter; for few of the trees in those parts are deciduous. Early shoots are never nipped by frost; the turf stays green,[1] and the flowers need only one morning's sunshine to show their faces. When our garden was under six inches of snow, lovely little climbing roses still swayed in the gusty wind on our trellises. Though somewhat pale, they none the less seemed quite pleased with themselves.

I had often gazed at the sea from the northern monastery door, and finally one day, when our invalid was well enough to be left by himself for two or three hours, my children and I set out to explore the coast in that direction. Until then the expedition had not interested me in the least, although my children, who ran like chamois, assured me that it was the most beautiful place in the world. Perhaps our visit to the hermitage, the original cause of all this sorrow, had left me with an excusable resentment, or perhaps I did not expect the view from sea level to be as beautiful as from the top of the mountain. At all events, I had not hitherto been tempted to venture outside the narrow vale of Valldemosa.

The Charterhouse, as I have already explained, stands at a division of the mountain-range, between the two broad-spreading arms of which a gently-sloping plain rises northward. When I gazed daily at the sea mounting to the horizon from far below this plain, both my vision and my judgement were remarkably at fault. I had not realized that the plain, after first rising, dropped abruptly at a point only a few hundred yards distant, and therefore imagined that it declined little by little to a shore some five or six leagues away. And indeed, how was I to know that the sea lay two or three thousand feet below us?[2] At times I was surprised at its loud roar, being, as I assumed, such a great way off, and failed to account for this phenomenon. Why do I often

[1] Between May and October in a normal year all the vegetation is burned up.

[2] It might have occurred to her that the fishermen could not have hauled their daily catch from a good deal farther away than Palma. And, as a matter of fact, the Charterhouse stands only about 1,000 feet above sea level.

laugh at the Parisian bourgeoisie, when my own surmises can be so extremely foolish? I had not grasped that the horizon, on which I used to feast my eyes, was fifteen or twenty leagues from the coast, whereas half an hour's walk would take me to the point where the waves broke. So when my children urged me to come and look at the sea, and said that it was only a few steps away, I never found time to humour them, thinking that what seemed only a few children's steps were, in fact, a few giants' steps; for we are all aware that children walk with their heads, giving no thought to their feet. Tom Thumb's seven-league boots allegorically express the fancy that children are capable of circling the world without noticing what they have done.

In the end I let them drag me off, convinced that we should never reach this imaginary coast, which I thought so distant. My son claimed to know the way; but since every way is the right one when you wear seven-league boots, and since for many years now I have shuffled through life in nothing but slippers, I protested that, unlike him and his sister, I could not take ditches, hedges and torrents in my stride. The next five minutes made it clear that we were not on the way *down* to the sea, for the rivulets were running fast towards us, and the farther we went, the farther the sea seemed to recede and the horizon to sink. I was convinced we were on the wrong track and resolved to ask the first peasant I met whether by any possible chance we might reach the sea if we persevered.

Under a clump of willows, in a muddy ditch, three shepherdesses, perhaps fairies in disguise, were shovelling muck in search either of some talisman or some salad. One had only a single tooth, and may have been the Fairy Dentue, who stirs evil spells into her stew with that fearful instrument. The second hag was, by all appearances, the wicked hunchback Carabosse, the deadliest foe of orthopædic institutions. Both grimaced hideously at us, and the first approached to snap her dreadful tooth in the direction of my daughter, whose youthful bloom quickened her appetite. The second tossed her head and flourished her mattock as if to deliver a swinge at my son's kidneys; evidently his straight, slim figure filled her with abhorrence. But the third, who was young and pretty, sprang nimbly to the edge of the ditch and, throwing her cloak over her shoulders, walked off and beckoned us to follow. She must have been a good little fairy, but in her mountain disguise liked to call herself *Perica de Pier-Bruno*.[1]

I met no friendlier native of Majorca than Perica. She and my goat are the only living creatures at Valldemosa who still keep a corner of my heart. Perica was coated with mud to a degree that would have made our goat blush; but when she had walked a short distance through the wet grass, her bare feet reappeared, not exactly white, but as dainty as those of an Andalusian girl, and her pretty smile, her confiding, quaint chatter, and her unselfish readiness to oblige, made us feel that we had discovered a pearl of price. She must have been sixteen years old, with delicate features; a face rounded and velvety as a peach; the anatomical symmetry of a Greek statue; a waist of reed-like slenderness; and bare arms tanned to a dark brown. Her hair escaped loose-flowing and tangled, like a filly's tail, from beneath a coarse linen *rebozillo*. Perica led us to the end of her field, and then across a meadow strewn with boulders and edged with trees; the sea had now completely disappeared, which made me think that Perica was playing a mischievous joke on us, and we were climbing the mountain again.

At the farther end of the meadow, however, she suddenly opened a wicket gate from which a path wound about a huge sugar-loaf rock. We followed its turnings and, as if by magic, found ourselves looking down through an immense void at the sea shore, apparently a league below us. This unexpected view made me giddy, and my first reaction was to collapse on my haunches. But gradually I conquered my fear and plucked up enough courage to follow the path a little farther, although it had been designed for goats, rather than humans. The sight before my eyes was so beautiful[2] that this time I had swallows' wings, not seven-league boots; and I set off past the tall limestone pinnacles that stood like giants, fifty and eighty feet tall, lining the crest of the cliff, trying, as I went, to peer down to the bottom of a cove

[1] Probably: *Perica de Ca'n Per Bruno*, 'Perica from the House of Peter Bruno'.

[2] It was here that Gustave Doré did his famous illustrations for Dante's *Inferno*.

which formed a deep hollow on my right hand, and on which the fishermen's boats seemed hardly bigger than flies.

Suddenly nothing was left before or below me but the pure blue sea. The path had wandered away somewhere on its own; Perica was shouting from above and my children, who were following me on all fours, began to shout even louder. Turning, I saw my daughter dissolved in tears; so I retraced my steps to ask what was the matter, but realized after a moment's thought that the children had good reason for their terrified despair. One step more, and I should have descended only too quickly, unless I had managed to walk upside down, like a fly on the ceiling; because those rocks jutted out over the bay, and the base of the cliff was deeply eroded. The thought of the danger into which I had led my children frightened me dreadfully and made me climb back hurriedly to them; but once they had been safely installed behind one of the gigantic sugar-loaves, I was again seized by a passionate desire to look at the bottom of the cove and the underside of the beetling rocks.

Never in my life had I seen anything like what I guessed must be below, and my imagination took wings. I descended by another path, clinging to thorns and hugging the stone pinnacles, each of which marked a new sudden drop. At last I began to catch glimpses of the enormous hollow, into which the waves dashed with a weird music, like the strains from some magic land, some unknown world that I felt sure I had discovered; until my son, frightened and furious, came and pulled me roughly back. I fell most unromantically not forwards, which would have been the end of my adventure and of me, but into a rational sitting posture. The child then scolded me with such eloquence that I abandoned my project, though not without a feeling of regret which still haunts me; for my slippers become heavier every year, and I do not think that the wings which I then found will ever again grow strong enough to bear me to shores like those.

There is no doubt, of course, that what we see seldom matches what we dream—I know this as well as anyone else—but the maxim applies solely to art and the works of man. I have found that whether because my imagination works sluggishly as a rule, or whether because God is more gifted than I (which is quite possible), nine times out of ten Nature is immeasurably more beautiful than I anticipate; on the few occasions that I remember having found her dull, I was in a dull mood myself.

Thus I shall never recover from the disappointment of not having climbed around the last rock. Might I not have seen Amphitrite herself ensconced there, beneath a vault of mother-of-pearl, her brow crowned with whispering seaweeds? All that I did see were limestone pinnacles, some rising from gorge to gorge like pillars, others hanging from cave to cave like stalactites, each assuming a strange shape and a fantastic posture. Above the abyss hung marvellously hardy trees, all deformed and half-uprooted by the winds; and from the bottom of the abyss another sheer mountain towered up to meet the sky: a mountain of crystal, diamond and sapphire. It was the sea which, looked at from a considerable height, creates the illusion of being a vertical plane; but I leave the explanation of this well-known phenomenon to scientists.

My children now conceived a desire to collect plants. The most beautiful liliaceae in the world grow among these rocks.[1] Between the three of us we finally succeeded in pulling up a bulb of crimson amaryllis,[2] though we discarded it before reaching home because of the weight. My son cut this wonderful plant into pieces to show our invalid a fragment, the size of his head. Perica, struggling with a length of kindling-wood which she had picked up on the way, and which with her sudden erratic movements, she constantly bumped into us, led the way back to the outskirts of Valldemosa. I enticed her to the Charterhouse, where I gave her a small present but had some difficulty in persuading her to accept it. Poor, sweet Perica, you neither had, nor ever will have, any idea of the good you did when you showed me that among those monkeys dwelt a gentle and delightful human being who was willing to help us without an ulterior motive! That evening we all felt cheerful, to have at least found one exceptional character before we left Valldemosa.

[1] Untrue.

[2] Probably a large *Scylla marina*, or sea squill, which, since it was not yet in flower, she mistook for the cultivated 'Lily of St. Joseph' from a similarity of leaf and bulb.

Chapter Seventeen

BETWEEN these two walks, our first and our last in Majorca, we had taken several others which I shall not describe, lest the reader be wearied by my enthusiasm for this everywhere beautiful countryside, strewn throughout with picturesque dwelling places, each striving to outdo the other: tumble-down cottages, palaces, churches, monasteries. If one of our great landscape painters ever visits Majorca, I recommend to his attention a country house named the Granja de Fortuñy, the vale of orange- and lemon-trees extending from its marble colonnades, and the entire extent of the road leading there. But without going so far as this, he could hardly take ten steps in that enchanted island and fail to pause at every bend of the path, now before an Arab reservoir shaded by palm-trees, now before a delicately carved fifteenth-century stone cross, now on the edge of an olive grove.

The sturdiness and outlandish shapes of some of these Majorcan foster-fathers are unequalled. The islanders declare that no olive plantation here is more recent than the time of the Romans.[1] I do not propose to dispute this, since I have no way of proving the contrary, even if the temptation came to me, and I confess it has not. After one look at the alarming appearance, the inordinate size and mænad attitudes of these fantastic trees, my imagination readily accepted them as contemporaries of Hannibal. When walking in their shade at dusk, you have to remind yourself that these are trees; because if you accepted the ocular

[1] It is difficult to destroy an olive-tree; its roots will sprout again even if buried under an asphalt tennis-court. But the Moors, not the Romans, planted most of the olive-groves.

and imaginative evidence, you would be terror-stricken by such fairy-tale monsters, some bending over towards you like huge dragons, with gaping jaws and wings outspread, others curled up on themselves like boa-constrictors, others again locked together in furious combat like giant wrestlers. Here a galloping centaur carries off a hideous ape on his haunches; there a nameless reptile engulfs a panting doe; yonder stands a satyr uglier than the he-goat with which he is dancing; and often one single cleft, gnarled, twisted, hunch-backed tree, which appears to be a group of ten separate ones, impersonates all these different monsters and joins again to form one single horrible head like that of an Indian fetish, crested with a solitary green branch. Anyone sufficiently interested to glance at M. Laurens's engravings need not fear that the appearance of his olive-trees is exaggerated. He could have chosen even more astonishing examples, and the *Magazin Pittoresque* (that amusing and unwearying popularizer of the wonders of art and nature) will, I hope, set out one fine morning to collect some of these.

Nothing less than Rousseau's[1] bold, majestic brush is needed to convey the grandeur of these sacred trees—which one expects every moment to break into prophetic voice—their rugged outline firmly drawn against the sparkling sky. (I must add that Rousseau, one of our greatest contemporary landscape painters, remains unknown to the public, thanks to the obstinacy of the academic selection committee, who have for several years denied him the right to exhibit his masterpieces.) The clear waters where asphodels and myrtles mirror themselves would bespeak Dupré. The severe Corot might be tempted by more formal scenery, where Nature, although uncurbed, becomes overdelicate and gives herself proud, classical airs. But to reproduce the charming tangle with which a whole world of grasses, wild flowers, ancient tree trunks and weeping festoons tent the secret fountain where storks wet their long legs, I should ask to have

[1] Theodore Rousseau, 1812-1867, called *Le Grand Refusé*, because his work was so steadily rejected by the anti-Romantic Paris Salon. He was engaged to George Sand's adopted daughter Augustine; but Solange made him break off the engagement by telling him, untruly, that Maurice had seduced the girl.

Huet's burin in my pocket, like a magic wand at my command.

Many a time, when I saw an old Majorcan Cavaller on the threshold of his yellowing, dilapidated palace, I recalled Decamps, the great master who raised caricature to the level of historical painting, the genius who could give wit, gaiety, romance, life in short, to bare walls! Those beautiful sunburned children who played in our cloister, dressed up as monks, would have highly amused him. He would have had monkeys there in packs, and angels among them, human-faced pigs, and equally dirty cherubs among the pigs; Perica, fair as Galatea, though coated with mud from head to foot like a water spaniel, and laughing in the sunshine like all that is sweet on earth.

But it is you, Eugène, my dear artist and old friend, whom I should have liked to lead up the mountain at night when the moon illumined the pallid flood. The countryside was lovely, and I was nearly drowned there along with my poor fourteen-year-old boy, yet he did not despair, any more than I lost the power of seeing how Nature that evening had become supremely romantic, supremely crazy, and altogether sublime.

He and I had left Valldemosa, during the winter rains, to go and fight the savage customs officials at Palma for possession of the Pleyel piano. It had been quite a fine morning, and the roads were passable; but while we busied ourselves in the town, the downpour started again, worse than ever. Here in France we grumble at the rain, yet we do not know the true meaning of the word: our longest rainfall lasts a mere couple of hours; one storm cloud follows another, and there is always a short breathing space between the two. In Majorca, a permanent mantle of cloud enshrouds the island, and remains settled there until it has rained itself dry; this may take forty or fifty hours, or as much as four or five days, without any break or lessening of intensity.

Towards sunset we climbed back into the *birlucho*, hoping to reach the Charterhouse in three hours' time. It took us seven hours, and we nearly spent the night with the frogs in the depths of some casual lake. Our driver was in a murderous temper; he had raised a thousand objections to setting out: his horse had lost a shoe, his mule was lame, the axle had broken—

anything you please. We now knew the Majorcans well enough not to believe him, and made him get up on his shaft where, for the first few hours, his face wore the gloomiest scowl imaginable. He would not sing, he refused our cigars; he did not even hurl oaths at the mule, which was a bad sign indeed. Evidently the iron had entered into his soul. Hoping to scare us, he had chosen the worst of the seven roads known to him. Since this one plunged lower and lower, we soon met the torrent, entered it, and did not emerge. The worthy torrent, finding its bed uncomfortable, had rolled out and flooded the road, turning it into a river whose seething waters charged us rapidly and with a loud roar.

When the evil-minded driver, who had counted on our faint-heartedness, realized that we were resolved to go ahead, he lost his temper and began to rave and swear loud enough to crack the vault of heaven and bring it tumbling about our ears. The hewn-stone channels which carry the spring water to Palma were so swollen that they had burst like the frog in the fable; and then, having nowhere to go, they had fanned out and formed first puddles, then pools, then lakes, and finally an inland sea which engulfed the whole countryside. Soon the driver had exhausted his vocabulary of saints and devils and did not know to whom he should now commend his soul. He got his legs soaked, which was only what he deserved, and found us little inclined to feel sorry for him. The conveyance was quite water-tight, and we were still dry; but every moment, as my son said, 'the tide was rising'. We proceeded blindly, horribly jolted, and every new pit we fell into promised to be our grave. At last we heeled so far to one side that the mule halted, as if to turn his thoughts heavenwards before breathing his last; the driver dismounted and scrambled up the bank of the road which rose to the height of his head; but he stopped when he saw by the gleam of twilight that this was the bank of the Valldemosa canal, become a river which, at intervals, spilt in cascades over our path, now also become a river on a lower level.

A tragi-comic moment. I had some fears for my own safety, and many for my child's. I looked at him; he was laughing at the face of the driver, who was standing straddled across the shafts, gauging the abyss, and now without the least desire to make merry at our expense. When I saw my son so calm and cheerful, I felt that he carried in him an instinctive knowledge of his fate, and regained my trust in God, relying on that intuition which children are unable to express in words, but which mantles their brow like a cloud or a ray of sunshine.

Seeing that there was no way of abandoning us to our unhappy fate, the driver resigned himself to sharing it, and became suddenly heroic. 'Don't be afraid, my children,' he told us in fatherly tones; then uttered a great shout, and lashed at his mule, which staggered, fell, rose, staggered, fell again, and finally stumbled forward half-drowned. The carriage heeled over, ('Here we go!' and 'Here we are again!'), lurched across to the other side but, with sinister creaks and prodigious leaps and bounds, emerged triumphant from the ordeal, like a ship which has touched the rocks without splitting.

It seemed that we were saved, and even still dry; but before reaching the mountain we made a dozen false starts on our nautical drive. When at last we came to the ramp which the monks had built, our mule, exhausted and also frightened by the noise of the torrent and the wind, began backing to the edge of the precipice. We got out and each heaved at a wheel, while the driver dragged the conceited M. Aliboron by his long ears. This procedure had to be repeated innumerable times, and after two hours' climbing, in the course of which we had not advanced half a league, because the mule had sunk to its haunches on the bridge, shuddering in every limb, we resolved to leave man, carriage and beast there, and reach the Charterhouse on foot.[1]

This proved no mean undertaking. The steep path was a rushing torrent which it needed all the strength of our legs to struggle against. Other smaller impromptu torrents would come roaring down from the rocks to appear unexpectedly on our right, and we often had to make a dash to skirt them or cross them at all hazards, lest they should suddenly become impassable.

[1] Having bullied the driver into making this journey, though he did all he could to dissuade her from setting out, she derisively abandoned him in that frightful gorge.

The rain fell in streams; enormous clouds, blacker than ink, ran across the face of the moon; whereupon, wrapped in greyish, impenetrable shadows, buffeted by the fierce wind, feeling the tree tops bending to touch our heads, and deafened by the sound of cracking firs and rolling stones, we were forced to halt and wait, as a poet once joked, until Jupiter had relighted the snuffed candle.

In the intermittent periods of light and shade, Eugène, you would have seen the most sinister and strange highlights and shadows, as earth and sky grew alternately bright or dim. When the moon beamed radiant again, and wanted, it seemed, to dominate the dark blue space cleared before her by the gale, the rain clouds would reappear like ghosts eager to enshroud the bright disk in their mantles. They over-ran her and would sometimes split apart to reveal her as lovelier and more helpful than ever. The mountain streaming with waterfalls and the trees uprooted by the storm were suggestive of Chaos. We recalled that splendid witches' sabbath which you once saw in some dream and sketched with a brush dipped in the red and blue waves of Phlegethon and Erebus.[1] And barely had we gazed at this infernal scene becoming real and flaunting itself before our eyes, when the moon, swallowed by the aerial monsters, vanished once more and left us in a bluish limbo, where we seemed ourselves to be floating like clouds, unable even to see the ground on which we risked our legs. At last we reached the cart track that led up the mountain, and were out of danger because we had by then put the waters behind us; though overwhelmed by exhaustion and practically barefoot. This last league had taken us three hours to negotiate.[2]

However, the fine weather returned and the Majorcan steamer was able to resume its weekly journeys to Barcelona. Our invalid did not seem fit to stand the crossing, but he seemed equally unfit to endure another week in Majorca. Our position was

[1] She probably means Avernus. Erebus was not a river.

[2] Her description of Nature's sublime beauties is difficult to reconcile with her statement in Chapter Seven: 'I have never met anyone whose enthusiasm for the beauties of Nature is more readily dulled by the slightest sensation of chilliness.'

most alarming; there were days when I lost all hope and courage. To comfort us, Maria Antonia and her village cronies in chorus regaled us with the most edifying conversations on the future life. 'That consumptive,' they used to say, 'will go to Hell, first for being a consumptive, and next for not going to confession.' 'Yes, of course. And when he is dead we shall not bury him in consecrated ground, and since nobody else will be prepared to bury him, his friends must manage as best they can. It remains to be seen how they will solve that problem. I shall have nothing to do with it myself.' 'Nor I!' 'Nor I: amen!'

At last we left;[1] but I have already described the company and hospitality we found on the Majorcan ship.

Once at Barcelona, we were in such haste to be done for ever with this inhuman race, that I had not the patience to wait for the formalities of our landing. I scribbled a note to the French naval commander stationed there, M. Belvès, and sent it to him by a dinghy. Almost at once he came in his barge to fetch us to his ship, the *Meleager*.

When we boarded this fine brig, as clean and elegantly kept as a drawing-room; and found ourselves surrounded by intelligent, pleasant faces; and received the generous and zealous attentions of the commander, the doctor, the officers and the crew; and shook hands with the worthy and witty French Consul, M. Gautier d'Arc—we jumped for joy on the bridge and cried from the bottom of our hearts: '*Vive la France!*' We felt as if we had been round the world, and come back to civilization after a long stay among the savages of Polynesia.[2]

Now, the moral of this tale, childish perhaps, but heartfelt, seems to be that man is not made to live with trees, stones, the clear sky, the azure sea, flowers and mountains, but with his fellow-men.

In the stormy days of our youth, we imagine that solitude is

[1] May 13th, 1839.

[2] This remark will read most ironically to anyone who has studied the story of nineteenth-century French colonial enterprise among the noble Polynesians; even if he has not had the privilege of living among the generous, honest and lovable Majorcans.

a sure refuge from the assaults of life, a certain balm for the wounds of battle. This is a serious mistake, and experience teaches us that, if we cannot live in peace with our fellow-men, neither romantic raptures nor aesthetic enjoyment will ever fill the abyss gaping at the bottom of our heart.

I have often dreamed of living in a deserted land, and every honest man will confess that he has done the same. But, believe me, friends, our hearts are too affectionate to live alone, and the only alternative left us is to live in mutual tolerance; for we are like children who, though they may tease, brawl, and even fight each other in the womb, can never part.[1]

[1] A reference to the Greek heroes Acrisius and Proetus, or to Pharez and Zarah in *Genesis*.

From

THE STORY OF MY LIFE[1]

by George Sand

. . . When I converse with the dead, I meet again—in the same sense of peace and the same hope of a better world where we may all be reunited under the rays of a livelier and more divine light than shines upon earth another soul,[2] not less beautiful and pure in essence, not less sick and troubled while in this world. I mean Frederick Chopin, who was my guest at Nohant during the last eight years of my retired life under the Monarchy.

In 1838, as soon as Maurice had been definitely confided to my charge,[3] I resolved to find a better winter climate for him than our own. My hope was to prevent any return of the cruel rheumatic pains from which he had suffered during the previous year. I also wanted to discover some quiet spot where I could make him and his sister work a little, and also work myself, though not to excess. One saves a great deal of time by seeing nobody and not having to stay up late at night. While I was making my plans and preparing to depart, Chopin, whom I saw every day and whom I loved dearly both for his genius and his character, told me repeatedly that if he were in Maurice's place, he too would soon get well; unfortunately I believed him. On this journey, however, I did not put Chopin in Maurice's place, but at Maurice's side. His friends had long been pressing him to spend some time in Southern Europe, because he was

[1] Published in ten octavo volumes by Michel Lévy, Frères (Paris, 1856). By this time George Sand could write more openly about her association with Chopin.

[2] She has been writing of Everard, an actor, now also dead.

[3] By her husband, Casimir de Dudevant, to whom the Court had awarded him after she had secured a legal separation. Maurice fell ill and his father, unable to face the responsibility and expense of a cure, sent him back to her.

thought to be consumptive; but Gaubert tested his lungs and swore that he was not. 'The fact is that you will save him if you give him enough air, exercise and rest.' And everybody else, knowing that Chopin would never make up his mind to leave the social life of Paris, unless he were dragged away by someone whom he loved and who was devoted to him, begged me wholeheartedly not to discourage so appropriate and unexpected a suggestion as the one he had made.[1]

It proved that I was wrong in yielding to their hopes and my own solicitude. Going abroad alone with two children, the elder ill, the younger exuberantly healthy and rebellious, would have been a sufficient undertaking without the added torment of heart and medical responsibility implied by Chopin's presence. But at the time his state of health reassured us all; or all except Grzymala, who was not far out in his diagnosis. Nevertheless, I begged Chopin to take careful stock of his morale, because it was several years since he had been able to face, with equanimity, the thought of leaving Paris, his doctor, his relatives, his flat and his piano. He was a man ruled by habit, and found the least change of circumstances a terrible trial.

I set off with my children, telling Chopin that I would stop for a few days at Perpignan, unless I found him already there, and that if he did not arrive after an agreed period, I should go on to Spain. I had chosen Majorca as our winter resort, on the recommendation of people who thought that they knew the climate and resources of the island well. Mendizábal, our mutual friend, a man no less excellent than famous, was returning to Madrid and offered to escort Chopin as far as the Spanish frontier if he really translated his dream of travel into action.

Well, off we went in November, my children and I and a maid.[2] We spent the first night at Plessi, where I joyfully kissed

[1] Mme d'Agoult had written to George Sand two years before: 'Chopin coughs with infinite grace. He is an irresolute man, whose cough is the only permanent thing about him.'

[2] 'Madame Amélie' was registered on the boat as travelling second class, while the family travelled first, and remained with them to the end of their stay. George Sand purposely omits all mention of her because (according to an unpublished letter in Señora de Ferrá's possession) she showed wicked treachery.

my mother Angèle and all the dear, good family which had opened its arms to me fifteen years before.[1] I found the little girls tall, beautiful, and every one of them married. Tonine, my favourite, was both superb and charming. The gout now obliged my poor father James to walk on crutches; and this proved to be the last occasion on which I kissed either him or Tonine, who died at about the same time as he did, while giving birth to her first child.

We made a wide detour, travelling for the sake of travel. At Lyons we met again our friend, the eminent artist Mme Montgolfier, Théodore de Seynes, etc., and went down the Rhône as far as Avignon, then on to Vaucluse, one of the loveliest places in the world, fit to be immortalized by a Petrarch. Thence, wandering through the South of France, we greeted the bridge of Gard, and stopped a few days at Nîmes for a reunion with our dear tutor Boucoiran, and a meeting with sweet Mme d'Oribeau who was to become my close friend. On the day after we reached Perpignan, Chopin arrived none the worse for his journey. The sea voyage to Barcelona did him no harm, nor that from Barcelona to Palma. We had calm weather and felt the heat increase hour by hour. Maurice minded the motion of the vessel hardly more than I did. Solange felt a trifle sick, but when the precipitous coast of the island appeared, shining under the early sun and laced with aloes and palm-trees, she began to run about the deck as joyful and fresh as the morning itself.

I have little to say on the subject of Majorca, having already written a substantial book describing my journey there and the anguish I suffered because of the invalid in my charge. As soon as winter came and announced its arrival by torrential rains, Chopin with equal suddenness showed every symptom of pulmonary consumption. I cannot guess what I should have done if Maurice had also been attacked by rheumatism. None of the Majorcan doctors inspired us with confidence and the simplest remedies were almost impossible to procure. Even the sugar was often of bad quality and made us feel ill.

[1] George Sand had become James and Angèle Duplessis' 'daughter' when ill-treated by her own mother, Sophie Dupin. The dear good family consisted of James, Angèle, and five daughters.

Thank Heavens, Maurice, braving the rain and wind from dawn to dusk by his sister's side, recovered perfect health. Neither he, Solange, nor I feared the flooded roads or the sudden freshets. We had found a deserted and partly ruinous Charterhouse, some cells of which made us a healthy and most picturesque home. In the morning I taught the children[1] and let them run wild for the rest of the day while I worked; in the evening we used to romp together down the moonlit cloisters, or read at home. The solitude was most romantic and we should have had a very pleasant existence there, despite the wildness of the country and the thievishness of the inhabitants, if the sad spectacle of our companion's sufferings and occasional days of serious anxiety for his life had not robbed me of all the pleasure and benefit afforded by our travels. This poor Great Artist proved a detestable invalid. What I had feared, though not with sufficient foreboding, soon came to pass. He grew completely demoralized. Though showing considerable courage in face of his physical decline, he could not assuage the terrors of his imagination. The monastery had been full of phantoms for him even when he felt well. But he never complained; I had to guess what ailed him. Once, when my children and I returned from our nocturnal prowlings among the ruins we found him, at ten o'clock, sitting at his piano pale as death, with haggard eyes and hair standing almost on end. It took him quite half a minute to recognize us. Then immediately he made an effort at laughter and played us the sublime things that he had just composed—and at the same time revealed to us the terrible, nerve-wracking ideas that had forced themselves on him in his hour of loneliness, grief and terror.

In such circumstances he composed the finest of his short pieces which he modestly called *Preludes*. They are the works of a master-hand. Many of them suggest a vision of deceased monks and the sound of funereal chants accompanying them to the cemetery. Others are melancholy and tender. They came to him in the hours of sunshine and good health, while the children were laughing under the window, and guitars twanging

[1] She mentions in a letter teaching Maurice 'Thucydides & Co.', and Solange the rules of indirect speech and the agreement of the particle.

far off, and birds singing in the wet trees, and little pale roses bloomed against the snow. Still others are of a bleak sorrow that charm your ear while breaking your heart. There is one, especially, which he composed on an evening of lugubrious rain and which depresses the heart to a frightening degree. We had left him well enough, that morning, Maurice and I, and visited Palma to buy necessities for our encampment. It took us six hours to travel three leagues through torrents swollen by ceaseless rain and reach the place where the floods were deepest. It was already pitch dark and we were shoeless and abandoned by our driver.[1] We hurried back, braving unheard-of dangers, because our invalid would be anxious for us; as indeed he was, but his anxiety had turned into a sort of quiet despair. We found him sobbing while he played his wonderful prelude. When we entered he rose, uttered a loud cry and said confusedly in a strange tone: 'Ah, I *knew* that you were dead!' After recovering his spirits and becoming aware of our plight, his retrospective view of our dangers made him ill. Then he declared that while waiting for us he had seen it all in a dream, and not distinguishing dream from reality, had calmed and as it were lulled himself by playing the piano, persuaded that he too was dead. He saw himself drowned in a lake, with heavy drops of cold water falling rhythmically on his breast.

I made him listen to the noise of the water dropping at regular intervals on the cell roof;[2] but he denied having heard it and even grew vexed when I described the phenomenon as 'mimetic harmony'. He protested violently, and with justice, against the puerility of imitating in music the stimuli of the outer ear. His genius was informed by the mysterious harmonies of Nature, which he translated into sublime musical equivalents, but not by any slavish transcription of external sounds. That evening's prelude was full of rain drops beating on the Charterhouse roof, but they were transformed by his imagination and singing gift into tears falling on the heart.

[1] In other words, the driver would not abandon his bogged mule and carriage to escort her home.

[2] This proves to have been impossible; it must have been the rain dripping from the roof into the garden.

Chopin's genius is the deepest, the most sensitive and the most emotional in existence. He made a single instrument speak the language of the infinite; often he could concentrate into ten lines, which any child can play, poetry of immense loftiness and drama of unequalled action. He needed no complex material means to lend his genius a voice: no saxophones nor ophicleides to fill the soul with terror; no church organs, nor *vox humana* to fill it with faith and enthusiasm. The crowd did not know him and still does not know him. Great progress in taste and artistic perception is needed before his works can become popular. But the day is not far off when they will orchestrate his music without changing his piano parts, and when all the world will recognize that though his genius was no less vast, complete, and learned than that of the great masters whose works he had assimilated, nevertheless his individuality remained even more exquisite than Bach's, more powerful than Beethoven's, more dramatic than Weber's. He is all three of them together, yet still himself, that is to say more delicate in his taste, more austere in his power, more piercing in his sorrow. Only Mozart is superior, because Mozart had also a healthy calm and therefore a greater fullness of life.

Chopin was aware both of his strength and of his weakness. His weakness lay in an uncontrollable excess of power. He could not paint a masterpiece with flat tints as Mozart—but only Mozart—could do. His music was full of unexpected nuances and, on occasions, bizarre, mysterious, tormented. Though he had a horror of the unintelligible, his excess of emotion carried him unwittingly into regions that he alone knew to exist. I may have been a bad critic for him—because, by knowing him so well, I had managed to identify myself with all the fibres of his being. For eight years, during which I was initiated, day by day, into the secret of his inspiration and musical brooding, Chopin's piano revealed to me the joys, obstacles and tortures of his thought. In the end I understood him as one understands oneself; a critic on less intimate terms with him might have insisted that he should be more generally intelligible.

Sometimes, in his youth, jovial and ingenuous themes had occurred to him: Polish songs and romantic pieces, of a charming gaiety and adorable sweetness, which have never been published. Even some of his latest compositions are like crystal springs in which the unclouded sun lies mirrored. But how rare and brief are these ecstasies of his quiet contemplation! The lark's song in the sky and the calm gliding of the swan over motionless waters are, for him, lightning flashes of loveliness in serenity. The plaintive cry of the famished eagle from the Majorcan crags, the harsh whistle of the north-easter, and the dreary desolation of the snow-clad peaks affected him longer and more deeply than the sweet perfume of the orange-trees, the gracefulness of the vines, or the quaint Moorish *cantilena* of the labourer's songs.

This was always his character. Reacting at times to the pleasures of affection and the smiles of Destiny, he could yet be chilled for days or whole weeks by the clumsiness of some insensitive person, or by the insignificant contrarieties of real life. And, what was so strange, a true calamity did not oppress him so much as a small vexation; it seems that he was not strong enough to take it in immediately or even suffer from an emotional reaction afterwards. Thus no close connecting link could be found between his emotions and the causes that provoked them. As for his deplorable health, whenever actual danger threatened, he faced it like a hero; yet worried miserably about small ups-and-downs; as is the history and fate of those whose nervous systems are over-developed.

Easily disturbed by pin-pricks, having a horror of misery, and a constant need of refined comforts, he naturally conceived a disgust for Majorca after a few days of illness; but was too feeble to retrace his steps. When he grew better, contrary winds prevailed, and three weeks passed before the Palma-Barcelona steamship, our only possible means of travel, though hardly qualifying even for this distinction, could leave port.

Our stay at Valldemosa was therefore torture for him and torment for me. Though sweet-tempered and charming in Parisian society, Chopin when sick and confined to the exclusive company of a few intimates, drove these to despair. No man could be nobler, more delicate, less selfish; more faithful and loyal in his dealings, wittier in his gaiety, more serious in his intellectual approach to problems, or more magisterial in solving those within his own domain. On the other hand, alas, none could be less constant in his moods, of a cloudier and more delirious imagination, of a more impossible touchiness and exigence. But one could not reproach him for all this; the fault lay solely with his sickness. Chopin's spirit was roasted alive: the fold of a rose leaf or the shadow of a fly would drain the life blood from his veins. Apart from me and my children, he found everything under the Spanish sky distasteful and revolting. Impatience for his departure nearly killed him; he felt the delay even more cruelly than the inconveniences of his enforced stay.

At last we managed to reach Barcelona and thence, when the winter had passed, sailed to Marseilles. I left the Charterhouse with mingled joy and grief. Alone with my children I could have happily lived there for two or three years. We had a trunk packed with good books of elementary education, and plenty of time for explaining them. The sky was becoming magnificent and the island an enchanted place. Our romantic setting charmed us. Maurice had grown visibly stronger, and so far as we three were concerned, privations made us laugh. I would have enjoyed wonderful hours of undisturbed work; while not acting as sickbed attendant I was reading splendid books of philosophy and history, and the invalid would have been adorably well-behaved had he been able to get better. With what poetry his music filled this sanctuary, even during his most painfully agitated moods! And the Charterhouse was so beautiful under its festoons of ivy, the valley so wreathed in blossom, the air of our mountain so pure, the sea so blue to the horizon's verge! I had seldom seen and never lived in a lovelier place, yet I derived little enjoyment from it. Not daring to leave the patient, I could make no more than a brief daily sortie with my children, and sometimes could not escape at all. Fatigue and sequestration had made me quite ill.[1]

[1] She suffered from rheumatism.

HISTORICAL SUMMARY

by Robert Graves

I FIND it difficult to square this account of the winter with Chopin's letters. Not only is there a curious disagreement between the two accounts of the Son Vent episode (see p. 48), but when writing to Jules Fontana from Valldemosa on December 28th, Chopin does not appear as a helpless invalid:

> Can you imagine me here between sea and mountains in a huge abandoned Charterhouse, in a cell with doors as wide as those of a Paris coach-house? Behold me without white gloves, without curled hair, but as pale as usual. My cell resembles an enormous bier, its vaults are covered with dust, its small window looks out on orange-trees, palms and cypresses. Underneath the window, in a Moorish alcove, stands my bed. The works of Bach, my manuscripts, notes and miscellaneous papers—these comprise all my worldly possessions. An absolute calm . . one could shout at the top of one's voice and nobody would hear. Briefly, I write to you from a mighty queer place. .
>
> Divine Nature, yes, she certainly is beautiful here, but she ought not to interfere with mankind, nor the mails, nor the roads. I have often travelled between Palma and this place, always with the same driver, never by the same road. One body of water pouring down from the mountains cuts a track, another coming from a different direction wipes this out. Yesterday's road ends today in a newly-ploughed field, and where we then had no difficulty in driving, we would now have to negotiate water and rocks on muleback. And what extraordinary vehicles are used here! They explain, my dear Jules, why there isn't a single Englishman in the island, not even a consul.

> Nature in Majorca is bountiful, but mankind thievish. Since the people never see foreigners they cannot decide what to charge them; giving an orange for nothing and asking a fabulous sum for a breeches' button.
>
> Beneath this sky one feels oneself pierced by a poetic feeling which seems to emanate from every object in the neighbourhood. Every day eagles wheel overhead, and nobody pays the least attention to them. . .

On January 12th he writes briefly that he has been enjoying Moorish dances and African sun, and has always before his eyes the blue Mediterranean. He mentions three compositions on which he is working: they will be ready to send in a few weeks' time. He adds: 'I don't know when I shall return; perhaps in May, perhaps later.'

Unless, then, Chopin is trying to deceive Fontana, he has been living an active and amusing life and will be perfectly content to stay at Valldemosa for another six months, despite difficulties of food, transport and domestic service.

Thus I come to the problem which has puzzled me so long: what made George Sand write so recklessly and cruelly about the Majorcans? The obvious reasons advanced are not enough. It is pointed out that she had been prevented by Chopin's ill-health from finishing her *Spiridion*, and forced to turn cook and servant, whereas he managed to get through a great deal of work. But if she loved him, and was loved in return, she should have rejoiced in her self-sacrifice; and the Majorcans could not be blamed for his consumption. Moreover, she spent only two months at Valldemosa, and claimed afterwards to have written most of *Spiridion* there. It is true, of course, that the nobility of Palma had given her no extravagantly warm welcome. Yet they did not fail to be polite, while by her own showing she behaved most oddly: she visited the Count of Montenegro's house, was indirectly responsible for what seemed irreparable damage done to a priceless map, and scurried off guiltily without a word of regret. In a small town, overcrowded with war-refugees, she expected accommodation suited to her style and purse, and quarrelled with the hard-working carpenters who could not give her order priority. What vexed her most, apparently, was the realization that the coldness of her welcome had been largely due to Chopin's presence. A small group of Liberals spoke French and read the Paris newspapers, and therefore must have picked up the much publicized scandal of her recent Italian honeymoon with Alfred de Musset, whom she was supposed to have seduced, betrayed and abandoned. They doubtless saw another victim in Chopin. It is known that a copy of her *Lélia* went from hand to hand and caused a deal of excitement. The majority, however, being Francophobes and staunch Churchmen, with a severely Catholic education, knew little, and wished to know nothing further, about her. It sufficed that she was a friend of Mendizábal's, whom they regarded as their personal enemy, and she seems to have made no attempt to disguise her republicanism. This attitude must have been galling to her, because she had become easily the most celebrated woman in France, and could carry things off there with a high hand.

She decided to leave Palma and try her luck in the Majorcan countryside. On her grandmother's estate at Nohant, now her own, she had enjoyed good relations with the enlightened post-Revolutionary peasants. But the people of Establiments did not open their arms to her, and the intensely conservative and religious Valldemosans saw in her only a domineering, cigarette-smoking, ill-dressed, irascible woman, living in open sin with a foppish piano-player, six years her junior, and teaching her children to be as bad Catholics as herself. Majorca is a small island and news travels fast; they must have heard a great deal of scandal even before she arrived there. This was the first French family to settle among them, and for the past fifty years the Spanish clergy had been denouncing the French for their godlessness, immorality and military aggression. Nevertheless, the villagers, being a generous and law-abiding society, seem to have tried to make their visitors feel at home, as the torchlight visit mentioned in Chapter Thirteen shows. All the thanks that their leader gets in the book is to be laughed at for his bad French. If George had made the trifling concession of sending her children to Mass on Sunday mornings, things would have gone better; but she had brought them up in the 'noble religion of philosophy' and taught them to despise the Church. This made her occupation of the cell particularly odious. It had been previously occupied by the reverend Father Nicolás, one of the monks whom, as Chopin joked, Mendizábal seemed to have ejected as a personal favour for himself.

Chopin, again, was an aristocrat who never disguised his contempt for the common people; the villagers will have described him among themselves proverbially as 'a man who expects you to doff your hat from three leagues away', and her as a 'shameless one who leaps out in anger like a stone from a crushed cherry'. Towards children, Majorcans show the greatest indulgence, but Maurice hotly championed his mother, and his precocious sketches made the Valldemosans uneasy, especially the Monastic Orgy, pinned up in the cell. And Solange offended their sense of propriety by wearing trousers and playing the tomboy, instead of busying herself with the needle, the catechism, and other useful tasks.

Added to all this, Chopin's presence seemed to constitute a physical danger. They were terrified of consumption, then an incurable disease, and believed, as they still do, that sickness is a divine punishment for ill-doing. They thought George Sand wicked to expose her children to infection; they would think the same today, and with reason unless strict sanitary precautions were taken. For them she was no *grand esprit*, she was an evil woman, perhaps a witch, without shame or maternal responsibility.

The moral rule in Majorcan mountain villages is strict and simple: a girl must not only be a virgin at marriage, she must have the reputation of being so. Any scandal that cannot be disproved prejudices her chance of getting a husband. If she has once gone astray, three courses are open to her: emigration, penitent celibacy, or to become the village harlot—shunned by all good women and despised by the men who visit her under cover of night. Her presence will be tolerated only if her rôle is discreetly passive and if she attends confession regularly. Divorce being impossible, married couples behave as though sincerely attached to each other, even though they are not, for the sake of good manners; and if adultery takes place, the guiltless spouse is as anxious to conceal it as is the guilty one. Until a few years ago in Valldemosa and the other hill villages, when a married woman was notoriously indiscreet, the boys would come by night and blow conches outside her house to shame the husband.

Solange does not figure prominently in *Un Hiver à Majorque*, which was written soon after their return to France, and before she had fully revealed her character. Though no more than eight years old, she seems to have played a leading part in the drama. So far she had been known only as rebellious, arrogant, lazy and a domestic tyrant who relied on violent displays of temper for getting her own way. George spoilt and idolized Solange, perhaps because she had paid such a heavy price to win custody of the children from their father, Casimir de Dudevant; Solange repaid George with the cruelty, deceit and greed that Casimir had bequeathed to her.

Even today, when a foreign family settles in an isolated Majorcan village, the difficulties of religion, social behaviour and diet are increased by that of language. It is safe to say that apart from the mayor, the notary, and two or three others, nobody in Valldemosa could speak Spanish, a language of which George had only a smattering,[1] and nobody at all could speak French; Majorcan being in use everywhere. Maria Antonia had come from the Continent, but since she enjoyed the confidence of the village, is likely to have been the daughter of some soldier once stationed in Majorca, else they would not have understood her. Majorcan is an ancient language, the basic elements of which no native of France, unless he or she happens to be a Southerner, can hope to pick up in less than six months of study; whereas George was from the North and her Nohant peasants talked the *Langue d'oïl*, as opposed to the *Langue d'oc*. But this rule applies to

[1] As Quadrado points out in a footnote to his *Vindicación*, the few Spanish phrases she uses are all incorrect, e.g.: *Es a la disposición de V.*; *El flor de su juventud*. If she had been able to string even a few words together, she would have had little difficulty in investigating the secret of fifteenth-century monastic life. A Carthusian priest still lived on the premises, disguised as a lay apothecary, and though she knew no Latin, he could not have taken Holy Orders unless he were fluent in Spanish.

adults alone: a French or even an English child can become fluent in Majorcan after a few weeks' residence. Maurice at fifteen was too old to do so; Solange at eight was not. Of the whole family, therefore, only Solange will have known what was being said in the kitchen, or been able to interpret between Chopin, her mother and Maurice on the one hand, and the Valldemosans on the other. This explains why Sebastian Nadal, who took part as a boy in the masquerade procession, writing sixty years later, had a clear recollection of Solange, but not of Maurice. (He remembered George principally because she used to write underneath a tree in the monks' cemetery and had a companion, the musician Chopin, who 'passed as her husband'.)

Now, it was Solange who, seven years later, engineered the fatal breach between her mother and Chopin by representing herself as his one true friend, and making him believe a series of revolting and scandalous lies. After eloping with a scoundrel named Clésinger, who was later to carve the bas-relief for Chopin's tomb at Père Lachaise, she told Chopin that George had encouraged Maurice to seduce his own adoptive sister, Augustine, then taken a secret lover (Victor Borie, a journalist), and encouraged Maurice to shoot Clésinger. She herself, she said, had been cruelly turned out of the house to make room for Borie.

A girl who lies like this at fifteen can hardly have behaved much better at eight. It is impossible to accept the picture of Solange as ministering angel which George has painted in *Un Hiver à Majorque*. Solange will have been bitterly jealous of Chopin, once he became the most important person in the household, the invalid who must be cosseted and humoured at all costs; and angry that because of him the village viewed the family not only as moral, but as physical, lepers. Yet she seems to have been clever enough not to let anyone, even Maurice, guess what game she was playing. I cannot believe that the Valldemosan children stole and then watered Chopin's milk; though they may have spilt it once, or even twice, and then filled up the measure with water. Neither can I believe that Chopin would have become so obsessed by the notion that monks' ghosts were haunting the cell unless this had first been suggested to him. And did the fleas on the roast chicken come from the kitchen? And who told George of the sacristan's reputation as a Don Juan? A more important problem, perhaps related to these, is: what happened between George and Chopin at Valldemosa to make her write to his friend, Count Grzymala, in the spring of 1846, that for the past seven years she had lived a virginal life with Chopin and with all other men?

While Maurice and their mother were in Palma buying food, or enquiring after the piano, or fetching it, Solange stayed at home; and a true ministering angel would have taken care that Chopin did not work himself into the pitiful state of nerves in which they found him. She was perfectly capable of scaring him with ghost stories. I can hear her whispering: 'Not a word to Maman, or she'll forbid us to go out in the cloisters after dark! But Maria Antonia *saw* that procession of monks carrying the coffin to the cemetery; she saw it as sure as I see you there. And one of them nodded to her and said in Majorcan: "Tell him to prepare for this!" What could he have meant, dear Frederick? And last Sunday morning in broad daylight, the *niña* saw a monk—it may have been Father Nicolás—sitting on your bed and frowning at Maman's underclothes. Promise me that you won't tell her! I'm your friend. I don't want to frighten her. You're different. You're a brave man.' She was equally capable of drinking the milk, to deprive Chopin of it and vex her mother, and then swearing that the village children were to blame. And capable not only of reporting the sacristan's love-life, but of telling Chopin that the sacristan had boasted in the kitchen of a 'new and important conquest', and asking what that meant. Capable even of collecting fleas from the ears of their tame sheep and goat, and putting them into the bed which Chopin shared with her mother; and, once, under the dish-cover when the roast chicken was served. And she will certainly have reported, with a pretence of philosophical scorn, what Maria Antonia and the other women were saying: that he was shameless to live with a married woman in a cell which had been for centuries occupied by holy monks, that he was a consumptive and would soon die—good riddance to him—and that, unless he repented of his evil ways, he would burn for ever in Hell. Long acquaintance with Majorcans has taught me that they would never have spoken directly to her mother or to Chopin on these subjects, even if they could have made themselves understood; but they would have felt it their duty to enlighten Solange on the seriousness of her position. And if she passed on all the gossip to Chopin and her mother, pretending innocence of purpose, this clears up several historical obscurities. Luis Ripoli's newly published *Chopin: Su Invierno en Mallorca* supports my theory by referring to a letter of Solange's; she gleefully describes how the chambermaid—presumably the *niña*—and herself dressed up in monks' habits, which they found in the monastery, and frightened Chopin out of his wits by creeping into the cell at dusk. Nor was this thoughtlessness: Pauline Viardot, the singer, has recorded that '*Solange fait le mal pour l'amour de l'art*'.

It must be remembered that the attraction between George and Chopin had been one of opposites. Chopin was a Catholic conservative; she was a Radical free-thinker. He loved her, but knew that his family would be scandalized if they heard that he shared a bed with a married woman, whose children slept under the same roof; and that she neither believed in a literal Hell nor allowed them to believe in one. Did he perhaps feel that the villagers' moral censure was, after all, deserved, and that the very monks were rising from their graves to warn him of his impending death and damnation—unless he repented? Did he, thereupon, seek out a priest and make his penitent confession in Latin? And did the priest answer that his only hope of salvation, if he could not do without George, was to live like a brother with her for the rest of his life—meanwhile trying to save her soul and that of her children? That would explain all the known facts, including Maurice's later resentment against Chopin for playing the virtuous part of *paterfamilias* at Nohant, and with Chopin's boast that he provided a wholesome background for the children who would otherwise have grown up as wild libertines. It would also account for Chopin's improved health in the middle of February, remarked on by George, his sickness having been to some extent psychological.

My impression is that Chopin's religious scruples, fortified by fear of death and Solange's terrifying whispers, caused him to take this decision; and that his relations with George were paradoxically strengthened by the restraint it put upon them both. Consumption is a disease that fosters rather than reduces eroticism, and Chopin may have forced a promise of faithfulness from her in return for a similar promise by him. At any rate, he continued to be intensely jealous of her male friends; and George, though a warm-blooded woman who, since her husband's betrayal of his marriage vow, had felt as free to take a lover as he was to take a mistress, loved Chopin. She even loved him enough to mother him chastely and accept his jealous suspicions, ingratitude, querulousness and moods of frigid politeness with the patience of a saint; allowing him to use Nohant as a sort of hotel, and even to treat her as his social inferior. It is remarkable that he never acknowledged his debt by dedicating a single composition to her, even the 'Waltz of the Little Dog', which she had suggested that he should write. This was dedicated to the Countess Potocka. The rest went to the Princesses Württemberg, de Beauvau, de Souzzo and Czernicheff; the Countesses Fürstenstein, Mostowska and Esterházy; the Baronesses Rothschild and Billing—and so on.

George could not blame Solange for her part in Chopin's return to orthodox morality, but must have felt her own acceptance of it as a dismal defeat—what she calls 'a sacrifice of self-esteem and rooted inclinations'. She therefore revenged herself in this book on the Valldemosan villagers, whom she held solely responsible for the step Chopin had taken. How dared they interfere with her private life by exerting pressure on poor sick Chopin, through her gullible daughter? She called them uncharitable, superstitious wretches, monkeys, cannibals, thieves and (most significant of the way in which her mind was working) the bastard children of lascivious and hypocritical Carthusian Fathers, whose main pleasure lay in seducing the married women who came to their confessionals.

Even in her description of Palma, most of which is at second-hand, she devotes two chapters to denouncing the inhuman cruelties of the vanished Dominican Fathers, and extolling the noble rage of the people who had risen up and destroyed their monastery—though she is aware that this was the work of a demolitions contractor. Nobody could mistake hers for sober historical criticism. She seems to be beating down Chopin's sentimental picture of monastic peace and, as again in her pretended reconstruction of the life of a Carthusian, displays a personal spite which can only mean that the monks have in some way injured her. When she writes: 'Religion is very powerful in Spain and, no doubt, more than one destroyer repented next day and made his confession to the monk whom he had just hounded out of the sanctuary', is this an indirect allusion to Chopin's backsliding from the libertarian principles she had inculcated in him? Did he perhaps make his confession not to the Valldemosan parish priest, or to some Cathedral Canon at Palma, but to one of the friars whom his friend Mendizábal had dispossessed? I should have guessed to the ex-Carthusian apothecary Gabriel Oliver, whom she accuses of selling his wretched drugs for their weight in gold. But Señora de Ferrá assures me that he was not a priest, only a simple monk.

Chopin never ceased to love George, but a misplaced trust in Solange—his acceptance of whom as his one true friend suggests gratitude for a timely reconversion—persuaded him that George was unworthy of a man's trust; and mother-love prevented George from telling him the ugly truth about Solange. He seems to have expected George to come and plead for his forgiveness which, of course, she could not do. The breach, therefore, remained unhealed, and when she eventually heard that he was dying, and wrote to his sister for news of him, the letter was suppressed. He died in the conviction that his deep and Christian love had been betrayed; and two days before the end he whispered reproachfully to his friend Franchomme: 'She promised that I should not die except in her arms.'

Long afterwards, Liszt, in whom Chopin confided, wrote that 'all the long-scattered rays of happiness were concentrated within this phase of his life. . . . The memories of the days passed in the lovely island of Majorca, like that of an entrancing ecstasy which fate grants but once in a lifetime even to her most favoured children, remained perpetually dear to Chopin's heart. He always spoke of this period with deep emotion, profound gratitude, as if its joys had sufficed for a lifetime, and without hoping that he could ever again find such felicity—in which the flight of time was marked only by the tenderness of a woman's love and the brilliant flashes of true genius.'

For Chopin, it seems, the Valldemosan episode held the fragrant memory of a secret spiritual victory over his baser instincts; but it reminded George Sand only of her humiliating abandonment of principle in accepting his continued love on terms dictated by the Church that she hated.

TO GEORGE SAND: A REFUTATION[1]

by J. M. Quadrado

ONE November morning, in 1838, the news spread through Palma that Mme Dudevant, whose literary name was engrossing France at the time, had arrived in our island. Enthusiastic young men proudly looked forward to reading in the famous novelist's features her character and spiritual nature, and the impressions which our delightful countryside and Gothic monuments had made on her. A small literary advanced guard, who were familiar with George Sand's name because of its constant occurrence in the newspapers, and had gone so far as to read her works, delighted in the honour paid Majorca by this visit, and persuaded everyone else to do the same. Genius is sincerely admired and respected in small isolated towns (as the Indians marvelled at Spanish ships until they learned their use and manner of propulsion) if only because the inhabitants are unaccustomed to see it prostituted. Nevertheless, the undistinguished lodging which she chose, her unwillingness to receive visitors, the cold words of disdain that were always on her lips, the rudeness shown the young Marquis of —— [La Bastída][2] for whom she carried an introduction, and above all the equivocal company she brought with her, suggested that she was embarrassed by society. No attempt was therefore made to dispute her preference for freedom and retirement, in which the Majorcan ladies were happy to leave her, being (if you like)

[1] From *La Palma: a Weekly Journal of History and Literature*, May 5th, 1841.

[2] Mme Dudevant owed this nobleman a thousand courteous attentions, but one day, when detained by urgent business and prevented from accompanying her to the Charterhouse, he offered her the escort, instead, of his distinguished uncle, besides the freedom of his house and carriage. This offer she refused, advancing some trivial pretext, but on the following day went to Valldemosa with another family. To complain subsequently of the Marquis's discourtesy is the very height of impudence.—J. M. Q.

backward enough to place morality before cleverness, and to honour themselves with the title of 'wife' rather than 'authoress'. In the hope of enjoying, let us say, a higher degree of 'relaxation' in the country than in the town, she withdrew first to a house in Establiments, and then to the Charterhouse of Valldemosa where (apart from some rumours which earned no greater attention than they deserved) little more was heard of her. In Palma the caprices of genius are neither worshipped nor commended, and a pretended disdain for society, shown by taking flight from it, is hardly the way to win its esteem and attention. Four months later the news circulated that Mme Dudevant had left; and the people of Palma, few of whom had been either able or desirous to see her, forgot that she had ever come to the island. The visit might still be remembered, for all they cared, in those country districts which alone had merited her attention; by simple villagers who, unversed in the principles of Romanticism, and alarmed by her habit of wandering through cemeteries at night, not only believed the lady to be a *Straniera*, but also formed certain other less kind and less superstitious judgements about her.

Two years passed, and no one doubted that such a long period, in a life strewn, like her novels, with amours and adventures, would have erased us from her memory as completely as she had been from ours; until, last January, the *Revue des Deux Mondes* published a virulent article attacking our beloved Balearic island. This was followed by a second instalment and a third: enough to make a volume for separate sale. It is not clear what caused the nervous hysteria in which these articles seem to have been conceived, or the anger which induced such uncivil jokes and absurd reflexions; or how she came to sully the brilliance of her language, as when a beautiful girl shows vexation by rumpling the clothes she is wearing—or as when the authoress herself walks out wearing men's clothes and enveloped in the smoke of her cigarette. Had we not watched her defend worse causes than those which these articles so elegantly support, we should lay down that aberrancies of judgement and literary bad taste almost always reflect depravity.

An implicit law—as ancient and universally accepted as those defending the rights of the people, and more than ever respected now that civilization has progressed and good manners have become general—prevents a private person, whatever his genius or standing, from indicting an entire society. It likewise prevents the peace from being disturbed, or honour offended, by private quarrels; or a nation from being provoked except by the voice of another nation; and it brands insults against which satisfaction cannot be demanded as acts of cowardice. This law, being bound to that of hospitality, has always been respected by travellers. Even their shrewdest satires contain no odious generalizations that break the bonds of humanity and make light of the truth and circumspection that should distinguish the honest writer. But to slander a peaceful people (who at the most could be charged with indifference towards her) by taking advantage of her own reputation, and of their remoteness and isolation; to write off with the stroke of a pen, as cowards, hypocrites, pickpockets, Indian monkeys, Polynesian savages and the like, more than 160,000 of our islanders, and further to extend the abuse to all Spaniards—to act thus was reserved for a woman as impudent and undependable in her words as in her actions, one whose audacious ways have put her 'outside the Law of Humanity', and who boldly claims the right of saying whatever she pleases, merely because there is nothing that cannot be said in print.

Moreover, although she specifies the reasons which brought her to this island, we cannot see in what way her desires and hopes were deceived. She came in search of Nature's delights, and found a pleasant countryside and magnificent views—superior, she admits, to those of Switzerland. She came in search of tranquillity and solitude; solitude and tranquillity she found about her in plenty. She came in flight from the press, and found here only the modest Palma *Diario* which, forgetting her resolutions, she deigned to read and comment upon. It would have been splendid to be pursued by glory, while fleeing from it; to discover her name engraved on remote beaches; to rest from the homage of Paris amidst other homage, the more flattering because more spontaneous and farther from its focus; to suffer the curiosity of a simple populace; to muse amid the sound of distant acclamations. But our honest islanders did not know what to make of these charmingly coquettish artifices.[1] Doubtless their negligence and lack of foresight has cost them dear. Europe's admiration could not console the famous authoress for the indifference of our obscure and as yet uncivilized islanders, and for the severe silence with which, smothering our admiration for wasted talents, we declined to join in the universal applause that encourages vice. This susceptibility has been a thorn in the flesh, reminding her how inconvenient was the journey, how startling our customs, how prosaic her experiences. Yet of what use is a romantic soul if it shrinks on encountering the least privation or opposition, if it cannot thrive but in the monotony of its own comfortable routine? Of what use are philosophy and tolerance if neither accommodates us to the habits, and even the obsessions, of the country whose guests we happen to be? Of what use is genius if not to cover up those egotistical trivialities and weaknesses which make us ashamed of mankind?

Is it so, then, that our fields are no better than untilled, barren wastes and serve only as pasture for the pig with which we victual Europe—the Golden Fleece, our whole subsistence, and the noble subject for the illustrious lady's jokes? Does the miasma of our olive oil cover the whole region (she declares that this is no exaggeration) like a poisonous atmosphere? Has the island really reverted in agriculture, in commerce, in industry, and in the customs of its inhabitants, to the days when slings whistled in the vigorous arms of our ancestors? It would be amusing—if we did not pity the abuse of such great talent—to note her perpetual ill humour and vindictiveness; the blunders with which anger makes her contradict herself at every step;

[1] Writing of the solemn welcome which Palma accorded to St. Vincent Ferrier in 1413, Mme Dudevant observes that Miss Fanny Elssler, were she to hear of it, could not refrain from smiling. We must confess that since this celebrated dancer has received such extraordinary acclaim in the capital of the United States [*sic*], the authoress of *Lélia* and *Jacques* can reasonably take it ill that she did not earn an equally warm welcome here. But though unfortunately we no longer live in an age when a people can be stirred to its depths by the arrival of a holy missionary, we still need several years of progress before we can offer a similar reception to any: 'Pilfering girl or damsel on the prowl.'—J. M. Q.

the roundabout ways in which she persistently turns the praise she cannot avoid bestowing on us into castigation; the tediousness with which everything in Majorca is made to look exotic, insupportable and absurd—even the January rains. But do not hope to disarm her by logic: do not point out that a scarcity of passengers obliges our steamship to pay its way by shipping cargo as well. ('No, no: why should it transport pigs from Majorca? Is not Mme Dudevant coming aboard with her invalid?') Do not explain that since she engaged nearly all the cabins she should of course have expected the voyage to be dearer. ('Scandalous greed on the part of the captain!') Or that we do not need iron roads for our pack-animals which carry the limited trade of the interior. ('Horrible precipices that offer only Death!') Or that ready-made furniture is neither to be found nor hired, because the local population is static, and no immense caravans of over 6,000 travellers enter and leave the city daily, as in Paris. ('The laziness, the stupidity of your workmen!') Or that our temperate climate makes window-panes and fireplaces scarcely necessary, though they may be found in any house of moderate comfort.

But why go into all this? When she describes those four dank, bare walls, reeking of oil, those foetid camp-beds, that food consisting largely of garlic and peppers and seasoned with vermin, we cannot do less than admire her ingenuous economy. For some reason or other she was content to lodge in a common eating-house, though the city boasts four respectable inns; and then lamented the lack of zeal shown by her cicerones, or her evil star, that landed her in a quarter, inhabited by ruffians or gipsies, recalling those ulcers of London and Paris, described by Sir Walter Scott in his *Fortunes of Nigel*, and Victor Hugo in his *Notre-Dame*. To be thus exiled from good society, to find every door closed in an island famous for its hospitality; to find oneself without shelter and shivering as though beneath a blanket of ice even in a new and comfortable house; to make hearts and houses freeze at one's approach: for this to happen one must surely bear a brand on one's brow, or live in the perpetual shadow of misfortune.

We may be wrong in treating these newspaper articles more

seriously than was intended. What is not intended to be viewed except through the spectacles of fantasy, necessarily looks shapeless and unnatural to the eyes of truth. If she tells of palm-trees swaying above every farm; of the very Arabic, very melancholic, songs with which our women sing their children to sleep; of portentous grape clusters weighing twenty-five pounds; of scenery more Alpine and imposing than that of Switzerland, no less delightful than that of Italy, more luxurious and virgin than that of Louisiana—we, who are not unacquainted with our country's charms, nor inclined (if I may put it that way) to consult a disdainful stranger on the worth of our treasures, will nevertheless thank her romantic pen for having perfected the picture—and even created it at times. But if among these opulent and privileged fields she paints you a picture of the stupid, needy Majorcan mending his stockings or mumbling his rosary, or singing *Ave Marias* as lullabies to his pigs—which are dearer to him than his children; or makes the whole crew of the steamship, led by their captain, rise up at night to whip the herd of swine and thus distract them from seasickness; if she presents you with a grotesque dance at which every onlooker, including the Mayor bearing his staff of office, squats on the ground in Oriental fashion; if she recognizes bacon as the sole basis of our culinary art; if she regards as our native fare dishes never presented at any decent table; if she allows her pen to record vile expressions only excusable in a drinking-den—then laugh at those innocent pranks, applaud as much as you please the inventiveness of those Rabelaisian sketches and essays; and above all take care not to be more irritated by her pretty touches than by her ill-conceived caricatures, which rebound to the ridicule of the pen that consigned them to paper.

Palma's monuments and antiquities have occupied her merely in passing, perhaps because they seemed too numerous, or because archæology is not her *forte*, as some small absurdities convince us. Since all the historical or architectural fragments which she has inserted are borrowed from M. Tastu or M. Laurens, we owe nothing but the insults to her. On the one occasion when she was pleased to examine our curiosities, her flurry—however ingenuously she may disguise it—caused the irreparable loss of a cartographical monument which was worth somewhat more to Majorca than the honour of her visit. Of our Cathedral, marvelled at by foreigners, she remarks fleetingly that it contains hardly anything of stylistic importance, and that it cannot be compared with Barcelona Cathedral. She lavishes praise on the entrance halls of the principal houses; we believe the interiors would have pleased her no less but, since it is clear that she entered scarcely a single one, she must be relying on some guide-book or other when she describes the living-rooms as lofty, shadowy and bare, and omits the tapestries, the damasks, and profusion of gilding with which they are adorned. In other circumstances she might have written that they were imposing in their simplicity, and of gentle melancholy, that they invited tranquil meditation, and I know not what else besides, because romantic interpretations are her speciality; but on this occasion she found our drawing-rooms detestable, and would even have preferred them to be enlivened by the presence of dogs and cats—a singular taste indeed!

She complains that our buildings and their contents have been allowed to fall behind the times when, alas, all that we see nowadays are houses in the modern style, with recesses inside and balconies outside which lend a shelf-like appearance to the façade; when rickety, painted Parisian furniture everywhere replaces the robust and handsome pieces of two hundred years ago and those charming inlays, so esteemed in France and such noble witnesses to the skill of our ancient cabinetmakers, which the authoress herself acknowledges. Nor does she stop here. In order to judge the character of a town, the influence of, and the relationship between, different social classes one has to conduct (or so it was once thought) a minute and prolonged observation based on continuous and varied intercourse. Well, now, Mme Dudevant, after her ten days' stay in the capital, remarkable for its complete isolation and more than complete disdain of our anthropology, has discovered the secret of local society, the mechanism which engages all its parts: it is, she explains, that our spendthrift noblemen sell themselves to diabolically covetous usurers who in turn dominate the peasants! She owes little gratitude indeed to the unnamed guide—was it perhaps merely her distraught imagination?—who has been ignorant or malicious enough to make her look so foolish.

Here, Madam, we have no Indian caste system. Here we have a middle class sufficiently powerful to pass you by in silence, and to destroy that feudal character which you have lent our city. Here a nobleman does not employ servants of a different sort from those employed by commoners, nor more of them than his modest revenue and estates permit; nor are they under any other protection than that shown by all generous masters to their servants when they grow old. Here, as happens in every country, wealth, talent and sometimes virtue are valued and respected; but nobility never, unless it is distinguished by one or more of these appendages.

Our fastidious traveller finds it embarrassing to make her story agree with the reputation which, she confesses, Majorca has won for affability and hospitality, and with the honourable witness of her own friends. Perhaps, she says, the great influx of Spanish refugees extinguished hospitality by crowding the native population together; but though the number of foreign residents—no greater during her stay than when MM. Tastu and Laurens visited us—might send up prices, it could never alter the Majorcan character nor change decent people into savages. And if she attributes that 'apparent' cordiality to the ties of interdependence uniting the classes, what prettier mechanism can there be, for those who do not understand disinterested virtue, than that which, with a single generous impulse, mobilizes an entire society in the service of travellers who carry letters of recommendation to it? We cannot reconcile with our alleged boorishness the courteous but hypocritical offers of hospitality also here attributed to us—surely we do not excel the Parisians in this respect?—though, indeed, she might well have found among us a greater degree of sincerity, had she thought fit either to ask for or to deserve this. And what astonishes me most of all is her passionate disdain of the labouring classes and peasants. Did this democratic female evangelist suddenly remember that she was the Baroness Dudevant? Did the fair *Valentina* fail to find among those virgin souls a single *Benedict*? Did the woman-parliamentarian come across no workman as wise as the one in

A Companion on the Tour of France, to take the road with her? But, of course, at that time she was absorbed by the sickness of a certain 'member of her family', whose exact position in the household some lingering scruple prevents her from defining, despite the careless arrogance of her generalizations.

Grief always encourages injustice; so we should not wonder when she calls [Señor Gomez] the owner of a house, 'savage'—and, by the way, he is no Majorcan, far from it—because he did not want it infected by a dangerous disease which this prudent lady bequeathed him. She now revenges herself by disguising its nasty nature. Nor should we wonder that she asks every peasant to feel the same gush of 'charity' for her own languid *Stenio* as she felt, and expose himself unnecessarily to what he believed to be contagious, though the patient was already in such good hands. In Majorca, too, consumptives die in the arms of mothers or wives, and their sickbeds are not deserted by friends; and here love and simple charity will defy death; but, as for one who pays with crude insults the disinterested services of an unhappy woman [Maria Antonia], who receives favours as dues, who publicly jeers at the faith and the quaint customs of villagers—nobody would be surprised to hear that her house was given a wide berth and that she was pointed out as one accursed of God.

Well, Madam, we may be fanatic and superstitious, but pray be consistent at least and do not suggest that we are vandals who tear down monasteries. We refuse to accept the glory you confer on us, or to acknowledge the regeneration thus allegedly inaugurated; we beg you not to dwell on the one blot in our history, the day of our disgrace! Do not tell artistic France, the France that owed its Renaissance to religion, that we broke like a toy what had been the glory of our ancestors: that we assaulted the august church where her artists had once assembled in admiration. The hard facts are those which you refuse to credit, but which history will reveal as true, namely that 'this deed of violence was carried out before the eyes of the horrified people by a few revengeful and greedy malcontents', and that nobody has since dared to declare himself responsible for it. The French should certainly be in no doubt as to the power that an authoritative and audacious minority can impose upon a nation. Your little piece, *A Monastery of the Inquisition*, says this well enough, and we forgive you the shockingly ill-conceived characters, the cunningly contrived declamations, the 'poetic licences', though they are far more licentious than you suppose —all these, for the sake of your message that 'artists cannot believe in art unless they also believe in religion', and for the moral, which amounts to this: 'A condemned criminal rejoices in the burning of an entire city, if he is thereby enabled to escape personal punishment.'

We shall avoid pursuing you into the realm of politics, or disputing your love for Señor Mendizábal, in which you need not fear many rivals; but content ourselves with quoting for the derision of Spaniards these words of yours: 'Mendizábal was a man of principles rather than of action, one of those generous and eminent spirits who sacrificed his personal interests to those of Spain.' And we shall offer one other passage for their loathing: 'When the Spanish people blushed at their own degradation and, despite their love of Catholic ceremonial, their reverence for monks, their idolatrous attitude towards these images and relics, found sufficient strength of heart and hand to destroy the latter with a more abundant faith in human rights than in any religious creed, they were greater on that day than is generally known.' We cannot make out what greatness lay in burning God's churches and the tombs of their fathers, in cutting the throats of harmless priests at the altar's foot, and then tossing up into the air this blood and these ashes. Nor can we understand how a woman of genius finds it possible to utter these phrases, unless it be that such ferocity is nearly allied to mental degeneration, and that the bacchante is twin to the harlot.

But you are mistakenly judging the nineteenth century by your own circle of private acquaintances, if you are shocked to find among the brambled crags of Valldemosa the yet living remains of monasticism, and of 'those sacrifices to a jealous God who needed human victims'—especially now that you need not leave Paris to see this same genius sheltered and reanimated under the mantle of the 'Inquisition Friars'. Not everyone has snapped the thread of faith which bound the fifteenth and nineteenth centuries; in the latter, as in the former, there are still evils to flee, passions to stifle, crimes or calamities to deplore; and if you reckon how massive those walls had to be, and how ancient and apparently dead that tree before the breath of regeneration could reach it, you will understand that until your arrival at those sacred precincts, no heart had ever palpitated in 'a hell of remorse and rebellion, philosophical doubt and superstitious dread'. Nor had this shelter of sinners who came for expiation, and of innocents who sought to preserve their innocency there, ever been profaned by the brutal villainies which you so cynically offer either as a homage to, or a vengeance upon, your own experiences.

In vain you ask those walls to reveal the secrets of monastic life. That secret is no farther than one's own heart and, so powerfully does the condition of the soul affect the senses, you should have grasped it yourself merely by a failure to discover in our austere Charterhouse the carnal voluptuousness of a Turkish seraglio. Your Lélia—and incidentally confess that however admirable this creature of your imagination may be, she is no match for the Blessed Catalina Tomás, a Valldemosan peasant girl!—even your Lélia, whom we mistakenly believed to be the product of your melancholic stoicism and your enigmatic soul, would have grasped this in her lucid intervals. You, however, looked on those monks with the eyes of a Pulqueria. Cannot you recognize that they needed a virtue wholly inaccessible to your black suspicions, if they were to deserve both the veneration of our 'malicious' peasantry, and the respectful silence about them which our Voltairean monkeys (if such exist) preserved in their anti-religious declamations, or the honourable exception which they made on these Carthusians' behalf? Cannot you recognize that some other motive than indolence or hypocrisy must have caused their submission not only to the austerities of the Rule but to the tedium and isolation that impressed you so powerfully?

That Rule may seem to you a brutal mode of congratulating a devotee, because there is, of course, nothing more ridiculous than virtue without hope of eternity; than expiation without repentance; than the repression of passions in one who lets his life centre upon violence. Call it, if you will, a robbery from humankind; diagnose an extinction of belief and feelings in those who devote their lives to God merely from a sense of charity for their suffering neighbours.—But you? What tears have you swallowed? What wounds have you healed? Whom have you made happy with your novels? Do you believe that they are food for the soul of man, or that God considers Himself rewarded by the flourishes of your imagination? You too have felt the need for retreat, but souls that are inferior to society try to escape from it as often as those that are superior; misanthropy or egotism guided by philosophy, and religious zeal or expiation guided by faith, seek shelter in the same wilderness.

Did you not realize that there were two sides to this question, when you were presented to the octogenarian hermit from whose 'hideously sottish countenance' you averted your eyes, but who was followed to his tomb by the veneration of the Majorcans? Why did you not realize that this dumb scene epitomized the science of Reason (or the pride of the stye), when, after paying virtue the obol of your insulting pity, you marched away in self-congratulation? And, after all, why not congratulate yourself (knowing that the secret of social destiny has been confided to you) that you are the apostle of that 'revolutionary church' founded on the sublime principle of labour, and manifested by the impersonal cult of the machine which must one day unite all nations under a single name? You can make a parade of defiance to persecutors and tempests, because your faith is destined to die not by lance-thrusts but by hisses, and because your phalansteries can always shine in the chorus of an opera, or the opening chapter of an historical novel.

Forgive us Majorcans if we have judged your doctrine by its evangelist and if, keeping before our eyes the nasty spectacle of a being without faith who cast a terror-stricken glance into that abyss, we cling more closely than ever to our ancestral religion. You have here attacked our towns and villages which, replete with simple faith, 'are said to retain' hospitality, sincerity, poetry and all the ancient virtues; and, smothering the truth under philanthropic calumnies, you have presented us to Europe with a sneering: 'This is Catholicism!' Very well, take the least loyal of our believers and display yourself to him saying, for a change: 'This is Philosophy!' It is not likely that he will choose the wrong doctrine.

We thank you for those kind words about our perfectibility, and reciprocate your wishes for our happiness. At your present height of perfection you will find many others to whom you can stretch a hand in succour before reaching us poor folk again: who have no desire to understand or honour God in any other manner than we do at present. Nor do we excuse ourselves, by pleading an all-embracing love of humanity, from loving and helping individuals; though, by so doing, we may risk exclusion from the banquet of liberty to which you invite us, and be cast into outer darkness. As for your missionary visit, it should have been prophetic and portentous: in Greece you would have been proclaimed a Pythoness; Chaumette would not have disdained to elect you his Goddess of Reason; and the followers of Saint-Simon will be blind if they do not recognize you as the Woman Messiah.

The vigour and energy of this refutation would be at variance with my name and years, were it not that I speak on behalf of a whole society—and this must always be of greater importance than any individual whatsoever. We do not flatter ourselves that our voice, raised from a rock in the Mediterranean, will resound in all those places where your opprobrium of us has circulated, still less that it will dissipate the black vapours with which so seductive a mouth has begrimed our reputation; but none will deny us the right of self-defence. Many readers will be found to side with this triumphant genius in her outrage against justice, and to charge us with impudence because our words are cruel. Let her then make a public complaint: 'I have been misunderstood; my heart bleeds from the buffets of gross men'—that same heart which I myself would once have ransomed with my life-blood, believing that it breathed the frustrated tenderness and melancholy pity of a Jean-Jacques Rousseau, but which today I do not think deserving of a single tear, because it conceals all the aridity and cynicism of a Voltaire.

Now let those who feel one drop of generous blood course in their veins, those who associate with the word 'fatherland' whatever is dear to them upon this earth, read her verdict that: 'The Majorcan is a savage who cheats, extorts, lies, abuses, and plunders to his heart's content, and would eat his fellow-man without a qualm were that the local custom; but who, despite his vices, is no more to be hated than an ox or a sheep because, like theirs, his spirit is lulled in animal innocence.'

Let them read this and then blame us if, inflamed by our indignation, we proclaim the truth locked in our breasts for two years past, as doubtless in many others throughout Europe, but which it is high time to publish at last: 'George Sand is the most immoral of writers, and Mme Dudevant the most obscene of women!'[1]

[1] Don José Quadrado later regretted 'having answered George Sand in the crude style employed by herself'. The original manuscript of *Un Hiver à Majorque* is even cruder than the version published. We are told that 'Dr. Marshmallow', who came to visit Chopin at Son Vent, 'was so filthy that our invalid could not bring himself to allow the man to take his pulse'. And that 'Don Gomez was the most filthily ugly man to be found in the four quarters of the world'